VGM Opportunities Series

OPPORTUNITIES IN OFFICE OCCUPATIONS

Blanche Ettinger

Foreword by
Jerome Heitman
Executive Director
Professional Secretaries International

VGM Career Horizons
a division of *NTC Publishing Group*
Lincolnwood, Illinois USA

ST. PHILIP'S COLLEGE LIBRARY

To the revered memory of Dr. Estelle Popham, a giant in business education—teacher, advisor, and friend.

Cover Photo Credits:
Front cover: upper left, Continental Bank photo; upper right and lower right, IBM photos; lower left, photo courtesy of Kelly Services, Inc.

Back cover: upper right, Hewlett-Packard photo; upper left, Beneficial Management Corporation photo; lower left, photograph supplied by White Office Systems, Division of White Storage & Retrieval Systems, Inc., Kenilworth, New Jersey; lower right, Bronx Community College photo.

Library of Congress Cataloging-in-Publication Data

Ettinger, Blanche.
 Opportunities in office occupations.

 (VGM opportunities series)
 Bibliography: p.
 1. Clerical occupations. I. Title. II. Series.
 HD8039.M39E77   1988   651.3'7'02373   88-60908
 ISBN 0-8442-6522-5
 ISBN 0-8442-6523-3 (pbk.)

Published by VGM Career Horizons, a division of NTC Publishing Group.
© 1989 by NTC Publishing Group, 4255 West Touhy Avenue,
Lincolnwood (Chicago), Illinois 60646-1975 U.S.A.
All rights reserved. No part of this book may be reproduced, stored
in a retrieval system, or transmitted in any form or by any means,
electronic, mechanical, photocopying, recording or otherwise, without
the prior permission of NTC Publishing Group.
Library of Congress Catalog Card Number: 88-60908
Manufactured in the United States of America.

8 9 0 BC 9 8 7 6 5 4 3 2 1

ABOUT THE AUTHOR

Blanche Ettinger is a professor and deputy chairperson in the department of secretarial studies at Bronx Community College of The City University of New York and has been teaching in the business education program at New York University. She formerly taught on the high school level; prior to that, she was a secretary to the executive vice-president of Cohn Hall Marx Company.

She received her B.A. degree and M.S. in education from Hunter College of The City University of New York and an Ed.D. in business education from New York University, where she also took many courses in guidance and occupational information.

Dr. Ettinger is recognized nationally for her contributions to business education. Active in professional associations through the years, she has served as president of the Business Education Association of Metropolitan New York, The New York State Association of Two-Year Colleges, Office Technology/Secretarial Educators of SUNY, and the Alpha Xi Chapter of Delta Pi Epsilon (honorary graduate business education fraternity). She also has served as editor of the spring 1985, 1986, and 1987 *Journal* of the Business Education Association of Metropolitan New York; member of the editorial board of *Educational Dimensions,* the professional journal of The New York State Association of Two-Year Colleges; PLS certifying board member of the National Association of Legal Secretaries; national council delegate of the Alpha Xi Chapter, Delta Pi Epsilon; and program co-chairperson of the 1986 annual conference of the Eastern Business Education

Association. She is also an active member of the business/education committee of the Association of Information Systems Professionals.

In recognition of her leadership, scholarship, and contributions to the field of business education, in 1987 at the annual convention of the Eastern Business Education Association, Dr. Ettinger was named the EBEA Educator-of-the Year; in 1982 she was the recipient of the Paul S. Lomax Award sponsored by the Alpha Chapter of Delta Pi Epsilon (NYU); and in 1979, she received the Estelle L. Popham Award by the Alpha Xi chapter of Delta Pi Epsilon (Hunter College). In 1982 Dr. Ettinger received the very prestigious Delta Pi Epsilon National Research Award.

Among her recent publications (some with co-authors) are: "Basic Skills and Core Competencies" (1989), *Keyboarding Proficiency Drillbook* (1988), *Time It! Drillbook* (1988), *Machine Transcription: Language Skills for Information Processing* (1984), *Opportunities in Secretarial Careers* (1984), and three previous editions of *Opportunities in Office Occupations.* In addition to writing for many professional journals, she conducts workshops and is a guest speaker, moderator, and panelist throughout the nation.

FOREWORD

From "bits" to "bytes," "RAM" to "FAX," it's a new language that we speak. While not the language of a particular country or ethnic group, the terminology is nonetheless spoken by a large body of people: the personnel in today's fast-paced office environment. For today's office employees, the new terms are more than mere words. They are a language of change—changes that, in the past decade, have transformed various aspects of office life.

With computers becoming commonplace, the flow of information in and among businesses has increased to phenomenal levels. High technology and the information age are dramatically modifying the traditional roles of office support staff. Companies are shifting more and more information-processing responsibilities to administrative workers, demanding exciting new skills and eliminating many mundane activities. For the career-oriented administrative worker, the changing American officeplace spells a world of opportunity.

Career-oriented? Previously, the term was rarely linked to office support staff. But under the language of change, it has new meaning. "Career-oriented" means training, planning, and taking advantage of a host of new opportunities created for clerks, secretaries, bookkeepers, receptionists, and other administrative employees in today's workplace. It means mapping out your future and assessing the tools you need to achieve your goals. And it's what this book is all about.

Opportunities in Office Occupations is a practical, in-depth, and invaluable source of information about trends and requirements in the office of the eighties . . . and beyond. Not only does Blanche Ettinger explain the skills needed to accomplish an administrative job today, she also pinpoints expectations for the future, the attitudes and aptitudes that can lead to success. What can you expect in the way of salary and promotional opportunities? The facts are clearly stated, along with tips about getting a foot in the door.

As you study the statistics, quotes, and straightforward, sound advice within these pages, we invite you to form new ideas about traditional professions. You can gain a sense of respect about your own career decision and the role of office support positions in today's businesses. Now more than ever, skilled office personnel are being sought to perform multifunctional duties within the corporate environment. Managers have come to respect and rely on support staff who can efficiently operate expensive, high technology gadgetry in a way that helps increase overall productivity of the entire office. They recognize the need for ongoing education among their staff and will reward those who show progress, professionalism, organization, and the ability to effectively handle large amounts of information.

The expansion of service-oriented (versus product-oriented) industries calls for office personnel who have, or can demonstrate development of, strong interpersonal or "people" skills. Administrative and clerical staff who meet these criteria can be quickly bound for the upward track.

Riding the upward track means learning the language of change—not merely the technical jargon, but the factors driving the changes in the American workplace. It means knowing the choices available, planning your career and goals, and being prepared through personal and technical skills to meet the challenges of the changing office environment. Obtaining your first administrative or clerical position can be one of the best places to begin and grow.

> Jerome A. Heitman
> Executive Director
> Professional Secretaries International

INTRODUCTION

The rapid advances in technology have impacted our social and economic environment. Changing demographics are reshaping the work force and the labor market. Economic forces necessitate that America maintain its international competitive position in world markets. As America progressed from an industrial society, the numbers of individuals working in offices in business and industry increased. The nature of the jobs in these offices has been impacted by technology, and many of these jobs are now in semiautomated environments where people and computers interact.

Changes are occurring in skill requirements, home-based employment, job availability and career ladders, new position categories, job responsibilities, organizational structuring, the physical environment of the workplace, and the use of computers and software for work processes. Sometimes jobs are modified through the addition or deletion of tasks which could also result in a change of boundaries between jobs. For example, certain boundaries between clerical and professional and between clerical and managerial may change when keyboarding is no longer relegated strictly to clerical staff. Similarly, clerical workers will perform tasks previously designated professional. Professionals might type their own drafts and memos, and secretaries might use on-line databases and statistical software to collect data. The major staffing problem will be an adequate supply of educated, trained workers.

In response to technological change, the demand for routine clerical jobs will decrease, and a premium will be placed on the need for higher-level cognitive and reasoning skills. Sex is no longer a barrier. Equal employment opportunity legislation and enlightened management now make it possible for minorities to move into supervisory and managerial positions, particularly in firms that have established information systems.

This sixth edition of *Opportunities in Office Occupations* is designed to reflect the many changes occurring in offices and to prepare individuals for clerical positions. It is addressed to high school and college students as well as to the maturing age group who may be reentering the job market or looking for a second career. This book will make you aware of the job market—the opportunities, duties and requirements of the job, necessary educational preparation, work situation, employment trends and earnings, and predictions for the next decade. You will be able to make wiser career choices after reading this narrative on office employment, for you will be able to assess your own interests, abilities, and values as you proceed in your search for a satisfying career.

CONTENTS

About the Author iii

Foreword v

Introduction vii

1. **The Opportunities and Trends** 1
   Profile of the labor force. Occupational employment implications. Opinions of business leaders. Effect of automation on clerical demand. Automated communication of numbers and words. Trends in office environments. Telecommuting. Unionization of clerical workers. Integrated office systems. Projections for 2000. Equal employment opportunities. Changes in age and gender of clerical workers. The kinds of clerical positions in which men or women are still predominant today. Employment perspectives of working women. Employment prospects for older workers. Classifications of workers in the clerical occupations.

2. **The Clerk** 49
   Changing activities of the clerk. Computerization in the office. What skills are important? Educational

Opportunities in Office Occupations

preparation. Community colleges. Company training. Educational institutions and corporate partnerships. Abilities required in tomorrow's offices. Beginning the search for a job. Employment testing. The working situation. Alternative work patterns in a technological society. Disadvantages. Promotion opportunities for clerks. Types of equipment commonly operated by clerks.

3. **Records Management: File Clerk to Records Manager** 85
A total systems approach. Employment and salaries. Educational requirements and personal aptitudes. The future.

4. **Information/Word Processing: The Secretary** 93
Employment outlook for secretaries. New innovations in recruitment. Salaries. A decade of change: what secretaries say! The changing role of the secretary. Promotion opportunities for secretaries. Limiting factors in secretarial careers. Educational preparation. Specialized secretarial jobs. Professional organizations in the secretarial field.

5. **Information/Word Processing** 116
Organization of a word processing center. Skill requirements and duties of personnel in word processing centers. The information processing specialist. Reactions of management to word processing. Reactions of secretaries to word processing. Salaries. Is shorthand on the way out?

6. **The Bookkeeper-Accountant** 131
Educational requirements and personal aptitudes. Educational preparation. The bookkeeper in the automated office. How to get started. The working situation for the bookkeeper. Salaries. Accounting

careers. Testing program. The working situation for accountants. Employment outlook for accountants. Sources of information about professional accounting careers.

7. **Processing Data by Machine** **147**
A look at the trends. Implications for career planning. Where electronic data processing jobs are found. Specialized data processing jobs. Educational preparation in high school and beyond. Employment projections. Salaries. Women in data processing careers. The road to success.

Bibliography and Recommended Reading **159**

TELLER
Go Home Smiling

FEE PAID Agency
OPERATORS
$14,300
p. office of int'l.
ders seeks exp'd.

ediate opening for te
.. with clerical exper
. If you have a bubblin
nality and enjoy work
ith people — have w
opportunity for you.

STOM SAVINGS
clerk

WORD PROCESSING SPECIALIST

- COMSAT has an immediate need for a word proce
ing specialist within the International Communicatio
Division. Responsibilities include producing correspor
ence, reports, statistical and technical documents,
proposals and contracts, and using AMTEXT wo
processing equipment.
- Requires a high school graduate or equivalent with
wpm typing, 3-5 yrs. experience at the operator lev
plus 2 yrs. as a specialist, machine transcription exp
ence, familiarity with AMTEXT word processing equ
ment, and ability to work under pressure. Overtim
required.
- COMSAT offers a competitive starting salary as wel
liberal fringe benefits, including retirement, medic
dental coverage, stock purchase plan, savings p
Credit union, etc. Interested applicants should call
Senior Employment Representative 554-6060, D

A ENTRY CLERK

entry clerk
in the McLean
o perform data
functions on a
uter terminal
Typing speed
wpm is required.
ound in data
sing is helpful but

TYPIST

Excellent opportun
for a good typist
work in convenie
downtown locatio
Accurate typing an
spelling and a pleasar
speaking voice are re
quired. There will be

n 11 a.m. an
in interview.

OFFICE AUTOMATION

Minimum of 5 years experience in required in application and integration of
information processing equipment into a Federal Government environment.
Familiarity with applications such as correspondence control, electronic mail
and management status reporting is highly desirable. Experience
ety of office automation systems and minicomputers is desired.

TYPESETTERS AND PROOFREADERS WANTED
Rapidly expanding
is looking

GENASYS offers an excellent benefits program to include 3 week
an educational assistance program and a profit sharing/retire
es should send resume or call

GRAPHICS

MANAGER, AUTOMATED SERVICES

We are seeking a motivated, responsible individual to superv
manage our account analyse, account reconcilement, & speci
computer services department. This person will manage daily o
tions, & insure proper staff training & motivation, & assist in
business development. Must have supervisory experience &
verbal communication skills.

HELP WANTED

CLERICAL

CRT OPERATOR

immediate openin
CRT operators
e day shift. Exp
e with CRT and t
equired. Excell
ensation and be

DATA ENTRY OPERATOR—We
are seeking a CRT operator to
become a member of one of our
tech indexing teams. Working
closely w/team members indiv
will be responsible for entering
indexing data using an on
tech CRT. We require CRT exper

TYPIST
Flex-time—it's here

Processing Department has had a Fle
Time program installed with a great deal of succes
& we offer you the opportunity to participate. T
successful candidate will transcribe from the lat
Dictating equipment for many of our key personn

To qualify for this position you must possess
- Typing 60 wpm accurate
- Good grammar and spelling

CLERICAL

PERSONNEL CLERK

We are looking for a mo
individual with good typin
office skills to fill a cleric
tion with the Personnel D
ment. Pleasant working c
tions and good salary for
individual. Interviews by ap

WORD PROCESSING OPERATOR
Washington, D.C. law firm de

CHAPTER 1
THE OPPORTUNITIES AND TRENDS

The changes resulting from office automation technology have been dramatic and have impacted the entire organization from entry-level clerical positions to top-level management. Many routine clerical positions are becoming things of the past, and unprecedented demands for information and increased productivity are major factors in the employment equation. Computers are entering every aspect of our lives from computerized cash registers to automatic tellers to industrial robotic systems. Technological trends that are changing job requirements are as follows:

- By the mid-1990s, every two or three office workers will share a terminal of some kind.
- Fewer lower-level workers will be needed in the clerical/support occupations, which will also reduce the number of first-line supervisors and managers required.
- A systems approach has become the mode for office activities.
- Jobs are becoming more interesting and now require the higher-level skills of problem solving and decision making as well as advanced technical skills.

A crucial part of a successful job search is the determination of employment opportunities and the awareness of long-range forecasts of personnel needs. The job market is different than it was even several years ago and will continue to change because of societal and technological developments. Shown on the facing page are ads appearing in current newspapers. These "Help Wanted" advertisements indicate the range of positions available for individuals with clerical and/or secretarial skills and reflect prevailing salaries. The discussion that follows in this book analyzes office jobs and job categories, the nature of specialized positions, educational requirements, conditions of work, earnings, personal qualifications, promotional possibilities, and projections for growth. Individuals interested in entering office occupations should be aware of the trends stated above so that they may plan their careers with vision and foresight.

At some time or other, most people hold some sort of clerical position in an office. It may be for the summer while the worker is in high school or college; it may be part-time after school, evenings, or weekends; it may be full-time and the ultimate career of the worker; or it may be a part-time job for the housewife whose family responsibilities permit work outside or inside the home only a few hours a week. Even if you are interested in finding a clerical position just for the summer or for part of the day, you can eliminate a lot of wasted motion by getting facts about the jobs in clerical occupations. Whether you are contemplating a long-term career or working as a clerk just for the time being, the only intelligent approach to the job is to consider its opportunities and limitations.

Clerical workers make up the largest of all occupational groups in the United States; however, there are conflicting views about the continued growth rate because of technological change. Some experts say that there is a declining growth in the number of office jobs; others believe that the number of office jobs will continue to increase because technology creates more jobs than it eliminates. Jerome A. Mark, associate commissioner for productivity and technology in the Bureau of Labor Statistics, points out that the pace of technology needs to be kept in perspective. He states that "even with 25 years of rapid growth in computers, there were, in 1980, still more hand bookkeepers in the United States than all workers in the computer-related occupations combined." However, a look at statistics reflects a slowing growth compared to the total labor force. In 1978, the U.S. Bureau of Labor Statistics reported that 16.5 million workers, or 18.2 percent of the total number employed, were clerical workers; in 1979, 17.9 million, or 18.3

percent; in 1980, 18.2 million, or 18.7 percent; in 1982, 18.4 million, or 18.4 percent; and in 1987, 18.2 million, or 16.1 percent. The large percentage drop from 1982 to 1987, as the figures reflect, is not due to a large decrease in the number of clerical workers but rather to an increase in total number of workers between 1982 and 1987. By the year 2000, moderate projections indicate that clerical employment will be 22.1 million, or 16.6 percent of the total labor force. (See Chart 1.)

In their article "A Look at Occupational Enrollment Trends to the Year 2000," George T. Silvestri and John M. Lukasiewicz report that the number of administrative support workers, including clerical, will increase more slowly than the average for total employment from 1986 to 2000, or only by 11 percent. This is in contrast to the 1972–1986 period in which total employment in this field grew slightly faster than total employment. In this group, total employment is expected to decline from 17.8 percent to 16.6 percent; however, two million jobs by the year 2000 should be created. Office automation and technology will probably cause a 14 percent decline in occupations such as typist and word processor and will create a growth in industries that employ clerical workers such as hotel desk clerks and new account clerks in banking. Other occupations expected to be affected favorably due to the rising use of computers throughout the economy are computer and computer peripheral equipment operators.

Chart 2 shows projected employment changes in occupations between 1986 and 2000.

More women continue to be employed in clerical positions than in any other single occupation. Currently, 80 percent of the clerical work force is female, and nearly one-third of all working women in the United States are secretaries and clerical workers. Women occupy only 7 percent of the higher-level managerial positions, and generally these jobs are in the lowest rungs of management. However, in professional categories such as accountant and auditor, the proportion of women who hold a larger share of these jobs will likely rise because of the great number of women graduating from professional schools. In 1983, more than 40 percent were accounting and business majors and 36 percent computer science majors.

4 *Opportunities in Office Occupations*

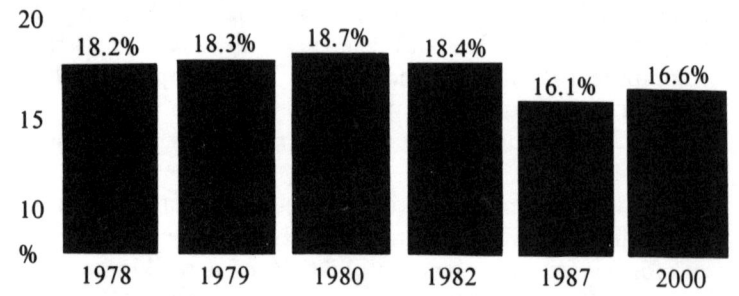

Wages also are likely to rise. The U.S. Department of Labor projects that by the year 2000 women's wages will equal 74 percent of men's.

CHART 2
Projected Employment Changes in Clerical Occupations
1986–2000

Percent Increase

Real Estate Clerks	39%
Hotel Desk Clerks	43%
Brokerage Clerks	28%
Receptionists and Information Clerks	41%
Interviewing Clerks, except personnel	45%
Computer Operators	47%
Peripheral Electronic Data Processing Equipment Operators	51%
Data Keyers, composing	51%

Percent Decrease

Typists and Word Processors	14%
Stenographers	28%
Payroll and Timekeeping Clerks	12%
Telephone Central Office Operators	18%
Telephone Directory Assistance Operators	18%
Procurement Clerks	13%
Data Entry Keyers, except composing	16%
Statistical Clerks	26%

In the past, women have been highly concentrated in clerical positions in government and in insurance, banking, and legal institutions. However, changes occurred with the introduction of automated equipment. For example, in the *insurance* industry, fewer tasks are performed by keypunch operators, bookkeepers, file clerks, mail handlers, and typists. Also positions for secretaries, filing, and other office clerks, bank tellers, telephone operators, and supervisory personnel are not increasing at the rate they once were.

In the *legal* field, a modest growth is projected in the employment of clerical support personnel. This is attributed to office automation. Word processing systems and computer software applications improve productivity in administrative functions, thus lessening the demand for new employees.

In a *banking* firm studied, the number of secretaries decreased; however, the content of the jobs improved so they were freed for activities that included customer contact and research. New career paths opened for those individuals who had acquired excellent skills with automated systems.

In *government,* of the one-quarter federal workers grouped under "General Administrative, Clerical, and Office Services," 8 percent fewer people are employed in these categories than there were in 1975. Certain job titles have disappeared since 1975, such as electric bookkeeping machine operator, calculating machine operator, and dictating machine transcriber. The number of secretaries in this group increased from 44 percent of the total employees in 1975 to 60 percent in 1983, while clerk-typists decreased by approximately 16 percent. The number employed as computer operators, specialists, and aides also grew considerably; however, individuals employed in these specialties were mostly men. Overall, the proportion of clerical workers in the federal government declined from 31 percent in 1975 to 25 percent in 1983.

On the brighter side, in three agencies of the New York City government, a study revealed that managers perceive less and less distinction between clerical and managerial workers. Increasingly, each group has assumed the duties of the other. Job content was changing, and apparently office automation increased the need for conceptual and abstract knowledge at all levels. Job content and promotional opportunities also changed; that could motivate clerical workers to gain and use their skills to advance to higher-level jobs. No statement was made concerning increase or decrease in demand for clerical workers.

In *advertising,* which once was predominantly the bailiwick of men, women are making strides. Generally, job opportunities exist in one of three main areas: 1) creative, whose employees are responsible for the conception and design of the ads; 2) media, whose employees evaluate, select, and purchase space in publications and time on television and radio for publicity; and 3) account service, whose employees act as liaisons between the agency and the client. In the last five years, women have moved into the account service sector and occupy approximately 50 percent of available positions. How do we account for this reversal? In an article by Philip A. Dougherty, "Women Are Moving Up in One Area," C. Kent Kroeber, director of human resources of the Interpublic Group of Companies, expressed his belief that this is attributable to the normal upward mobility of women in business, which is enhanced by their entering M.B.A. programs of study. Some perceptions about women reflect that they have proved themselves "superior to men," that they are "more buttoned up about their goals and objectives," and that the "younger ones seem to know more about the business."

Although technological innovations in information processing decreased employment opportunities for clerical workers such as payroll, filing, and statistical clerks; directory-assistance operators; and customer billing and inventory control clerks; there was an increase in the number of clerical workers needed to prepare the information flow for computers. Secretaries, receptionists and information clerks, general office clerks, and first-line supervisors and managers have not been adversely affected by computer installations. In fact, because clerical occupations are plentiful and have a high turnover rate, opportunities will exist, even in slow-growing occupations. Even though some occupations will employ fewer workers, most are expanding. Millions of jobs will be created in almost every type of occupation between now and the year 2000 because of an expanding economy and an increased demand for goods and services. According to the data compiled by the U.S. Department of Labor (reported in the *Occupational Outlook Quarterly,* Spring 1988), 21 million new jobs will be added by the year 2000, representing an average growth rate for all occupations of 19 percent.

Women need to take every opportunity to build their skills for newly emerging positions, which could open up avenues for upward job mobility.

Clearly, office automation will continue to change the nature and skill requirements of traditional office occupations. As this occurs, distinctions between men's and women's work and between clerical and professional work may become blurred, thus bringing about greater pay equity.

This manual is designed to give some concept of the vast field of clerical work—what kinds of jobs are involved, the qualifications for them, the salaries paid, the working conditions, and the possibilities for promotion. Hopefully, this book will give those who have only a vague notion about a "job in an office" a simple, realistic discussion of the clerical field. With an insight into the kinds of jobs available, the principal duties involved, the effect of technological changes on job classifications, the training necessary for clerical work and promotion opportunities, readers will be better prepared to decide either for or against securing a position in clerical work, one of the fastest-growing occupational fields in the United States.

Successful business operations depend on countless written records of facts and figures. The preparation and maintenance of these records require millions of man-hours annually. Those who specialize in handling these records are generally known as clerks. There are many kinds of clerks. A clerk who does many kinds of office work is a general clerk. A clerk who does a particular kind of office work is a specialized clerk. Some specialized clerical jobs are those of typist, receptionist, file clerk, bookkeeper, stenographer, cashier, postal clerk, shipping and receiving clerk, statistical clerk, stock clerk, and office-machine operator (duplicator operator, calculator operator, data-entry operator, and voice-writing equipment operator). Although the names of the jobs of specialized clerks do not always include the word *clerk,* they actually fall into the clerical classification of office jobs. The clerical field, as defined by the U.S. Department of Labor, covers a wide range of office occupations from messenger to the highly skilled positions of title searcher and examiner, executive secretary, or office manager with professional certification. This manual will consider the overall development of the clerical field and then discuss in detail the job of general and special clerk—with special chapters devoted to the work of the word processors (stenographers, correspondence and administrative secretaries), data processors (bookkeepers, accounting clerks, computer operators), and records managers.

PROFILE OF THE LABOR FORCE

The profile of the labor force, which is projected to increase by approximately 21 million, or 18 percent, between 1986 and 2000, is changing. This represents a slowdown in rate of growth which is based on the following trends: the "birth dearth" generation (1965–1978), the slower rate of growth in the participation rates of women, and the declining participation rates of men. For example, the data on women reflect that from 48.4 percent in 1977, the participation rates of women steadily increased to 56 percent in 1987; for men, from 77.7 percent in 1977, the rate declined to 75 percent in 1987.

A number of major factors will affect the composition of the work force:

- There will be a decrease in the number of young workers aged 16–24 and an increase in the 35–54 age group;
- One out of five new labor force entrants will be a minority youth;
- Women, minorities, and immigrants will account for approximately 80 percent of the net additions to the labor force;
- Immigrants will represent the largest share of the work force since World War I;
- Ninety percent of the new jobs will be in services.

The changes that are occurring have some very important implications for occupational employment.

OCCUPATIONAL EMPLOYMENT IMPLICATIONS

An imbalance will undoubtedly occur between labor supply and demand, particularly since there is a decreasing number of young adults entering the labor market. Also, many of them are inadequately prepared for what the jobs demand, for they are functionally illiterate; and a considerable percentage are deficient in the basic skills. Included in this group are the high school dropouts and pushouts who graduate with inadequate reading and writing skills.

In some instances, because of lack of workers, employers have turned to other sources of employees; namely, recently retired individuals and immigrants. These alternatives also have special challenges. Retired individuals generally lack the flexibility to adapt to rapid changes, are less likely to change occupations, to move, to undergo training, and may lack the skills needed in information occupations.

Integrating a non-English group of immigrants into the job market is extremely difficult—and at times not feasible. Many of the immigrants lack the skills in demand.

Industry needs employees who are well-grounded in the basic skills of reading, writing, communicating, and processing information. In many jobs, a higher premium will be placed on analytic, cognitive, and reasoning skills. In addition, employees have to understand the American social structure and the employee-employer relationship and develop the proper attitudes and appropriate work habits. In effect, new employees will have to be better educated and trained than some of our present workers. Where does the responsibility rest to educate and train the nation's youth and prospective labor force? Collaborative efforts among government agencies, industries, institutions, and educators are the key to addressing the problem.

If you are interested in office employment, make education and training a high priority and seek career advice from school counselors. Also investigate the sources available for enrollment in special programs. As you plan your future, keep in mind that work-related education and training are lifelong endeavors, for the average worker can expect to change careers three times during a lifetime.

OPINIONS OF BUSINESS LEADERS

Several business leaders were asked for their opinions concerning vocational opportunities for clerical workers and for suggestions to those considering positions in the field. Through their statements runs a common understanding of the great need for qualified clerical workers with good attitudes and self-motivation.

Mr. Richard Neitlich, former assistant vice-president of human resources at Metropolitan Life Insurance Company, forecasts many career opportunities with excellent salaries for individuals who think of office work as a career rather than just a job:

> "Office work offers challenging and meaningful careers to millions of people. There are literally hundreds of types of office careers, requiring a variety of skills and interests. Typing, keypunch, stenographic, analytical, mathematical, supervisory, and management talent are just a few of the skills that are called for in today's office environment.
>
> "Many office positions lead to highly paid, responsible careers. For example, the modern-day secretary is frequently called upon to act as an executive assistant. In addition to taking dictation, filing, and typing, today's secretary is expected to act as a receptionist, organize the boss's work, screen mail, handle routine inquiries, and take the initiative on a variety of other matters. Executive secretaries are much in demand, and they earn excellent salaries.
>
> "Training is an ongoing activity in the office of today. Throughout their business careers, most office workers will find themselves learning how to use new equipment, adopting new procedures, or being trained for new positions with added responsibilities. Many seek opportunities to develop themselves through after-hours self-study programs. Promotions are usually available to those who are willing to put in the effort that is required.
>
> "In many offices, most supervisors and managers have come up through the ranks from lower-level jobs by demonstrating that they can take direction, learn the work, and cooperate with others to meet the goals of their organizations. They are frequently the ones who have shown that they take pride in their accomplishments and motivate others to do the same.
>
> "Those who succeed in office work are usually those who think in terms of a career instead of a job. They think of where they would like to be in five or ten years instead of looking for immediate satisfaction. Thinking in these terms, they are more interested in advancement opportunities than in small differences in starting sala-

ries. They are willing to take the time to learn as much as they can about their work and the company for which they work. They strive to do the best job possible, and they accept responsibility for what they do. They respect the abilities of others and are willing to take constructive criticism both from their supervisors and their more experienced associates.

"Because of the interesting variety of assignments, today's business world is an exciting place to be. There is also a great deal of intellectual stimulation for those who seek challenge and comradeship for those who like working with others.

"In short, office work can be highly rewarding in terms of job satisfaction, personal growth, monetary recognition, and in the opportunities it affords to meet others with similar backgrounds, goals, and interests."

A former president of the New York Chamber of Commerce, Mr. Joseph A. Healey sees a bright future for responsible young people who are interested in clerical vocations and who have the necessary skills, habits, and desire.

"Every day in New York City over 70,000 clerical positions go unfilled. At a time when other fields have too many applicants for too few openings, jobs in the burgeoning field of the information handler go begging for bright, responsible, well-trained personnel.

"No one quite learns the basics of a business like the secretary through whose hands pass the important communications that turn ideas and concepts into action programs. Just as communication in personal relationships keeps those relationships alive and growing, so communication by telephone, letter, memo, and report keeps all departments of a business in close contact with one another.

"The information handler interfaces with every level of a company. But—most important of all—clerical personnel are usually the first company representatives the public contacts. They give that first impression that can spell the beginning of a satisfying relationship for the business and the stranger who comes to the door. The enormous importance of this first impression—another form of communication—can hardly be overestimated. The company's image often depends on that helpful phone conversation, that thoughtful welcome, the kind of question which puts the visitor at ease.

"From public relations to processing the most sensitive information, the clerical worker keeps a business running smoothly. Competent, sensitive clerical workers are among the greatest assets businesses possess. Many companies have recognized that through the equal opportunity programs which they have promoted over the last ten years, the clerical workers of the 70s are quickly filling the managerial openings of the 80s."

Dr. Irene Place, professor emeritus of business at Portland State College and an active member of many committees in business management organizations, such as Administrative Management Society and Association for Systems Management, emphasizes that the impact of technological development on our economy and on our personal lives led to new job opportunities that require a different set of skills and knowledge.

"We are living in an era of new concepts about personal freedom and equality. This is a time of marvelous inventions, instant communication, and rapid transit. It is a time of miracle drugs and long life expectancy. The quality and nature of education have changed accordingly, just as our personal needs and life-styles are changing. The mind-boggling scientific and technical developments that are nurturing these changes are based on tons and tons of data that are stored, moved, and processed in electronic devices that operate at the speed of light.

"As a result of the above, there are many new job opportunities, but they use new skills and knowledges which, because of their complexity, turn many people off. Instead of meeting the challenge of preparing for a role in a new, dynamic environment, many people just goof off. They drift and dream. Eventually they become human discards and join the ranks of unemployed, unemployable, and homeless.

"To decide how to invest one's life and the amount of time allotted to each one of us is a difficult task. There are so many choices; so many sidetracks of false leisure and artificially satisfied dreams in which to get lost. It takes an alert mind and perseverance to find a way through the maze of opportunities and challenges and to avoid snares and traps.

"It is not fair to blame schools for the personal development problems of today's young people. Schools cannot assume the entire burden of preparing individuals for life. Nor can the home do it, even when one has a good home. The task must be a coordinated effort between education, home, and self. Actually, the self is always in the driver's seat because the self makes the decisions one follows. Self-motivation, then, is a key factor here.

"Motivation is an inner drive that causes a person to act in a certain way. It is something that happens inside a person even when the need is external. Motivation goes hand-in-hand with purposeful work. Unfortunately, not everyone likes to work.

"A concept of work that underlies the foundations of the United States is called "the work ethic." This concept holds that work is good in itself and that those who work purposefully not only make a contribution to society but are happier and healthier people by virtue of the act of working. By working, they are participating in the ongoing process of living. That is, they belong to the mainstream of the human race instead of being flotsam caught in a backwater.

"The work ethic that says one should work and make a contribution in life is derived from the philosophy of Puritans who migrated to this continent from England. They advocated work because in pioneer days, hard and continuous work was absolutely essential to keep families from perishing. The urge to work was further strengthened by ambitions to improve the level of living in what appeared at that time to be a land of limitless opportunity—and freedom.

"We assume that most people want to become respected, participating members of the vast work force of this wonderful country. What are some of the general skills and aptitudes needed? Specific skills would depend, of course, on the occupation area chosen. A list of ten characteristics that were compiled in November 1987 are offered by Dr. Matthew Prophet, the outstanding superintendent of public instruction, Portland, Oregon. The list is summarized here and gives some idea of needs as identified by one who works closely with the problems of preparing today's young people for future occupations.

"Dr. Prophet says young people need:

1. A salable, specialized skill to use to earn a living and to do useful and productive work;

2. A basic thirst and hunger for learning; a restlessness to know and to keep on knowing;

3. The ability to communicate, to say what they think; to express thoughts and ideas clearly in writing as well as orally;

The Opportunities and Trends   15

4. The ability to listen to others and read their written thoughts with understanding;
5. The ability to learn and to apply the knowledge gained;
6. A clear set of standards and ideas to guide life; that is, principles by which to live;
7. The ability to disagree without being disagreeable and to respect the views of others without prejudice against those of different races or social classes;
8. A happy, optimistic nature. This comes, Dr. Prophet says, from educating the spirit and inner soul. It also comes from thinking positively with an uplifting, wholesome outlook on life;
9. Economic literacy, especially personal money management. Everyone needs to know simple economic fundamentals;
10. The ability to maintain physical and mental health and to control creature appetites and passions;

"Dr. Prophet concluded his ten points with the thought that learning is a pleasant, never-ending journey during which goals can be reached periodically. One should worry, he cautions, when not moving in that direction.

"In conclusion, let us agree that the blame for personal failures or lack of motivation is not necessarily in education or even in the home environment. It rests, in the final analysis, on one's own shoulders. Therefore, take charge of yourself. Take charge of your own destiny. Be your own person. Aim toward a useful, participative life where you find satisfaction from contributing. Become a useful member and a team player in the human race. Carry on with dignity, confidence, and purpose."

Adella C. LaRue, a former president of Professional Secretaries International, in an address given at the 1987 international conference in San Juan, Puerto Rico, entitled "Creating Our Future," focuses on understanding oneself and the society in which one lives. This philosophy supports some of the comments made by Dr. Irene Place in which she talks about the need for individuals to take charge of themselves. In her address, which appeared in the October 1987 issue of *The Secretary,* Ms. LaRue states that ". . . you have the ability and resources to overcome the obstacles preventing you from achieving the things you want. To create that future, however, takes knowledge and understanding of the world around you, of your profession, of the place where you work, and, most of all, of yourself. . . . Think of your own capacities—what you are good at, what you like, what skills you lack."

Carolyn Fryar, senior vice-president of Kelly Services, Incorporated, envisions the role of secretaries as becoming more challenging and with increasing responsibilities.

"Secretaries are now assuming the role of information managers in offices as computers allow access to information never before available. A secretary/information manager must know where to get the information needed, how to get it, and what to do with it once she/he has it. This new role requires more analytical and creative skills. Once acquired, these skills greatly expand the secretary's role within an organization, and the job becomes more challenging and diversified.

"People planning to enter the profession can take three positive steps to prepare themselves. First, develop a basic clerical foundation. Learn how to type, input letters, and perform mathematical functions. Second, take advantage of all technological and training opportunities. Third, practice. Put that training to use as much as possible.

"A good way to start a career is to work for a temporary help service. It provides many benefits for aspiring secretaries. An individual gains income to help pay for formal education and at Kelly Services, receives free training in office automation skills. The variety of work offered by temporary assignments gives insight into many types of companies and the business world in general. Students and individuals with no formal work experience can use this insight to help them make career decisions while gaining practical experience, which can be included in a résumé.

"As office technology continues to become more sophisticated and widespread, the secretary's role, undoubtedly, will continue to expand to a more skilled and more professional level."

Although office work is becoming more and more automated, some types of clerical positions will continue to increase in number while new job opportunities develop. Clerical workers can be assured of employment for a long time to come. For the highly competent, there will be opportunities for advancement to higher clerical positions and to supervisory and administrative positions in the clerical area.

EFFECT OF AUTOMATION ON CLERICAL DEMAND

This is an era of great scientific and technological advancement, and probably no word can cause more excitement than *automation*. This word is of interest to businesspeople, educators, youngsters still in school, and all those in the labor force—the employed and unemployed.

Those not informed about automation envision themselves being replaced by mechanical monsters that will take away their jobs. They forget, or are unaware of the fact, that the computer must be told what to do and how to do it. The brain of the human being is behind every piece of mechanical genius; human beings are responsible for the development of systems and procedures that will utilize the capabilities of the machines for maximum efficiency.

Automation is not something new. Technological changes have been occurring in human civilization ever since the invention of the wheel. Despite the increased efficiency from these technological improvements that make it possible to increase production with fewer workers, the U.S. Bureau of Labor Statistics estimates that by 1995 there will be 15 million more persons gainfully employed than at present. This is 14 percent above the 1984 level. This rise in employment will be primarily due to the increasing number of women seeking employment and the growing need for services. In addition to new jobs and opportunities, technological changes have created new comforts, and new possibilities for better, safer, and more enjoyable living.

It is also true, however, that technology is bringing, and will continue to bring, great changes which will demand adjustment on the part of both the employer and the worker. The federal government, business, and schools are cooperating to make this transition as easy as possible for those presently employed and for the workers of tomorrow.

Advances in microelectronics technology, particularly the silicon chip, and the rapidly growing integration of computers in the workplace have automated many office functions and have affected the positions of clerical workers. Because many clerical tasks have been automated, there is a decreasing need for telephone operators and clerks in the following categories: filing, payroll, bookkeeping, accounting. However, employment opportunities in office occupations have increased and have created such white-collar jobs as programmer, computer specialist, systems analyst, auxiliary equipment operator, console operator, tape librarian, proofreader, word processing center coordinator, word processing supervisor, data-entry clerk, administrative support supervisor, database administrator, records management specialist, information specialist, knowledge manager, systems coordinator, and chief information officer. The advent of these last two titles reflects the changes occurring in office occupations. For example, chief information officer (CIO) is a career aspiration for an individual who has expertise in buying, installing, and maintaining computer systems. As organizations are beginning to realize that computers are critical to high-level decision making, CIOs are being hired. Systems coordinator is the other position that is emerging in nontechnical departments. A systems coordinator is responsible for converting the manual systems to automated systems when computers are purchased and for training office personnel.

It is important for individuals who are preparing for office careers to realize that, in addition to computer literacy, many traditional jobs require office automation skills, too. A look at the help-wanted ads for positions such as accountant reveals that personal computing skills are required, often with knowledge of spreadsheets.

Small as well as large organizations have automated their procedures because of the declining costs of equipment. Office support staff, such as typists and secretaries, now are using computers, electronic typewriters, and word processors rather than electric typewriters. In his article "The Rise and Fall of Word Processing," John B. Dykeman reports that statistics indicate that an estimated 18 million personal computers exist in business today and 85 percent of the users perform word processing. What is important to remember, however, is that presently national standards do not exist for either equipment or software. Therefore, within the firm, incompatibility may exist and even more so from one organization to another. Keep this in mind when making a decision to terminate one job for another, for it might entail additional learning and training.

Business organizations require a flow of information on an almost instantaneous basis. To cope with this need, business has invested in automated data processing equipment. Recognizing the power of this equipment to give fast, accurate, and detailed data on which to base decisions, management continues to add new applications. Thus, clerical staffs continue to grow to handle the data that are fed into and retrieved from the systems. Increasingly, a greater premium will be placed on the speed and accuracy of the workers who handle the information.

Business has also invested in word processing centers to reduce costs and to increase office efficiency and productivity. This reorganization of the traditional secretarial job requires a more specialized clerical worker, a word processor whose output is subjected to new standards and measurements.

The more boring and tedious types of paperwork will be taken care of by machines, freeing office personnel for more interesting and creative work. The office jobs of the future will be more challenging, require greater skill, be more varied, and undoubtedly provide increased opportunities for promotion.

Skills such as typewriting, shorthand, and filing will still be in demand; however, employees who are most sought after by business and industry are individuals who are well-grounded in the basic language skills of reading, writing, and speaking, as well as listening and computing. Equally important are a positive attitude, flexibility, economic literacy, and good interpersonal skills. Higher-level and promotional opportunities will be more readily available to individuals who are creative and have the ability to think, solve problems, and make decisions. Upgraded jobs will require of the employee advanced degrees of skill and accuracy.

Since the average worker will change jobs several times in a lifetime, a strong foundation in the basic and vocational skills will enable the office worker to be flexible. This is the key to success in an automated world. Not all the necessary training can be given in the schools, but a knowledge of basic principles will make on-the-job training relatively simple. Most accredited schools have acquired automated equipment for training students.

Today, data processing is a huge industry in itself. Smaller companies which do not have their own computers have access to them on a time-sharing basis. (A company may own or rent its own computers; it may buy the use of time on somebody else's computer; or it may take its data processing work to a service center for processing.) Generally, these firms hire their own programmers who enter the data in leased computers. Still other companies have a smaller volume of work and find it more economical to continue to work by hand. There are still many opportunities for employment in such places. In other organizations, even when word processing centers were developing rapidly, not more than 20 percent of the offices had word processing installations.

AUTOMATED COMMUNICATION OF NUMBERS AND WORDS

Data communications, a term widely used in the modern office, is the movement of business information or data from one person or place to another by electronic equipment. Most data communications make use of long distance telephone lines and terminal equipment such as typewriters and magnetic tape.

This new process gives rise to a need for skilled clerks. Such a system accepts information at the point it is generated, moves it to the point of processing (computer), and then sends it to the point of use. For example, an airline reservation clerk at a remote point keys in a seat reservation to a central computer; while the customer is waiting, the clerk gets instantaneous confirmation in return. In another application, a branch office of an insurance company sends instructions about a claimant's policy to a computer at the main office that is 2,000 miles away. In these new communication services, the operator can also use a dial telephone to transmit and receive data by electronic means.

The clerk, like other office personnel, processes and communicates business information. The data transmitted eventually terminate in the hands of a person who will use the information; therefore, trained personnel are necessary to plan, organize, develop, and utilize such a system effectively. People, as well as machines, are vital in this communication process so that information that is processed by the computer can be moved to the proper place at a designated time and in the proper form. Clerical workers are essential in controlling the office function and must be skilled in handling the input and output of such systems.

In organizations with word processing centers, the flow of information begins with the word originator, who is typically the executive. This individual dictates reports, letters, or statistical information onto tapes or cassettes through an ordinary telephone or through a more sophisticated telephone system. A central recorder in the word processing center picks up the information, and office personnel use text-editing typewriters or personal computers to convert these communications into typewritten pages. Word processing systems may extend outside the firm to include: 1) the linking of dictation units and automatic typewriters at locations around the country; 2) the use of facsimile equipment to send documents over ordinary phone lines; and 3) electronic input to computerized data banks. Word processing specialists are needed to operate the system from origin of communication to printout, storage, and retrieval.

TRENDS IN OFFICE ENVIRONMENTS

Those aspects of office environments which are in a continuous state of change relate to systems, productivity, personnel resources, and employee/employer personnel needs.

Information processing systems vary from simple to sophisticated installations that incorporate many forms of office activities: word processing, data processing, telecommunications, photocomposition, and records management. Sophisticated systems to process and communicate information accurately and speedily are being integrated through similar electronic hardware. Information network systems that utilize data-entry terminals and minicomputers are also developing to facilitate resource sharing for users via host computers. The rate of growth is phenomenal and is opening up more and diversified career opportunities which require different attitudes, new technical skills, higher-level decision-making and problem-solving abilities, and new knowledge qualifications. A question pertaining to these new designs is: who will manage these systems? Undoubtedly, the person who will qualify will have to understand the broad concepts of office systems, management, and evaluation of productivity and personnel.

In his article, "Improving Productivity in the Workplace," Dr. T. J. Springer stresses that the human factor is crucial in improving productivity. Equally as important as money invested in the workplace is the "full appreciation for the role of the human element. . . ." "While it is possible to achieve improvements in productivity by concentrating on the efficiency of machines, buildings, and support systems, it is people who ultimately determine if and how much productivity can be increased." As for the human factor, Springer firmly believes that performance improves with the kinds of tools used and the ways and places in which jobs are performed. In essence, improved productivity results from "matching the tools, tasks, techniques, facilities, furnishings, and people to yield a synergetic system."

In "The Human Cost of Computing," Jim Hall-Sheehy offers a similar view when he argues that the computer is best understood as an enlargement of the human mind. "Computers are an extension of human productivity, not a replacement for it."

A 1987 national study of office environments conducted by Louis Harris and Associates, Incorporated, for Steelcase, Incorporated, also supports the above-mentioned trends. It found:

- Participation, contribution, challenge, and information shar-

The Opportunities and Trends 23

ing are more important to at least 75 percent of the workers than workspace and design.
- Office workers are satisfied with their jobs; however, their expectations have risen, creating a gap between what they want from work and what they actively experience. Pertaining to the connection between doing a job well and getting what one wants out of life, only 53 percent saw a great deal of connection in contrast to 62 percent in 1978 when the same question was asked.
- Office workers believe they are working at peak capacity. This has created a gap with executives who see room for improvement.
- The intangible benefits workers desire are being underestimated by executives.
- Two-thirds of the workers interviewed use a personal computer or terminal, and nearly half of the executives have one in their office. The median usage is three hours per day.
- Seventy-nine percent of all office workers interviewed work 40 or more hours per week; only 25 percent prefer the open plan. Those employees with higher incomes are more likely to work 45 or more hours.
- Office workers generally prefer that smoking in the workplace be restricted. Twenty-one percent still smoke in the work area compared to 35 percent in 1980.
- Only 56 percent of the respondents indicate that the quality of their working life has improved, in contrast to 70 percent in 1978. A gap exists here, for 79 percent of the top executives believe their quality of working life has improved.
- Eighty percent of the interviewees say good employee benefits are important, up from 64 percent.
- Seventy-four percent of the workers believe good pay is important.
- Sixty-two percent of the respondents believe that executives should hold staff meetings with all levels of staff; however, only 31 percent of top managers believe this is important.

Overall, there is a considerable gap between what office workers consider important and what they actually experience at work.

Predictably, top executives found their work situation far more satisfying.

One in five workers now uses a computer for five or more hours a day; therefore, office arrangement and privacy are important issues. Employees indicated that they want a participatory management style, and they are seeking further enrichment of the job.

A study of trends in office automation and their effects on office workers by Omni Groups Limited, entitled "Office Automation and You," revealed the following:

- Within a few years, seventy-five percent of support staff and word processing specialists will be using computers.
- Seventy-five percent of support staff use computers for word processing.
- There is increasing use of computers for time management and office communications. Within two years, computers are expected to be used by support staff for calendaring/scheduling and electronic mail.
- A range of computerized managerial tasks in 63 percent of the *Fortune* 1000 companies are delegated to secretaries and other support staff; namely, computer accounting tasks, database management tasks, electronic spreadsheet management, and computer graphics applications.

The Omni Group found that job applicants need computer skills to function effectively on the job.

TELECOMMUTING

An employment trend that offers an alternative to working in an office environment is *telecommuting*. Office employees are now "going to work" via telephone lines rather than by car, bus, or train. All one needs to install a hookup from office to home is a personal computer that is connected to a telephone by a modem.

Telecommuting, also known as electronic cottages, is feasible for individuals who work with information. However, before opting for this alternative, consider the advantages and disadvantages. The advantages include savings on clothing, food, and transportation costs; savings on time because traveling to work is no longer necessary; control over one's work schedule; the option to work full- or part-time; and the ability to handle daytime personal obligations, including family and community responsibilities.

Some disadvantages that need to be considered include the lack of daily social contact; the fear of losing career advancement; the concern about handling technological problems that might occur; the possible constraints on time and workspace as workloads increase; difficulty managing time because of interruptions; and perhaps lower compensation based on piecework.

Various reasons why companies establish telecommuting jobs include: to reduce turnover and to retain valued employees; to overcome staff shortages; to attract prospective employees; and to maintain productivity at a reduced cost, resulting from not having to rent office space or provide other facilities or services.

Among the companies which found that workers were more productive at home are Blue Cross/Blue Shield of South Carolina; Control Data, which originally set up such an arrangement for people with disabilities; American Express, which employs many handicapped people; and J. C. Penney Company in Milwaukee, Atlanta, and Columbus, which hires employees on this basis to take catalog orders.

In "Telecommuting: The New Way to Work," Richard W. Samson reports that forecasters predict that by the year 2000, 15 to 20 percent of the population will be telecommuting.

Offshore commuting is another practice being used by industry to reduce labor costs. Presently a few thousand clerical employees are in the Caribbean countries where they perform data entry. Other jobs are transferred outside the continental United States to the less expensive Third World labor forces. This is made possible by advanced satellite and telecommunications systems. The linkage to mainframe computers in the United States makes it possible for workers thousands of miles from here to perform keyboarding entries.

UNIONIZATION OF CLERICAL WORKERS

Up to the present time, attempts at unionizing office workers have not been successful. Several factors still make this difficult, especially the great flexibility of modern computer systems, which can reduce labor demand and shift office work that is performed electronically to other areas in the United States. Unions are trying to offset their overall decline in membership, which occurred as the economy shifted from manufacturing to services, by increasing their organizing efforts in the white-collar and service sector.

Now that changes are occurring in white-collar employment due to laborsaving technologies, will unions be able to organize workers in the service sector? As stated previously in this chapter, the evidence is inconsistent. A study conducted by Leonteif and Duchin in 1984 predicted that clerical employment would decline from 17.8 percent of the labor force in 1978 to 13.5 percent in 1990. In "Technological Change and Unionization in the Service Sector," Cynthia B. Costello reports that a study by the National Academy of Sciences concluded that clerical employment would decrease 2 percent of its share of total employment by 1995. Both studies concur that the growth rate will be slower in the clerical occupations over the next decade than in the past.

The impact on the quality of clerical jobs is also controversial. Though automation makes obsolete certain skills, it does create a need for others. But which trend will prevail? Is it really preferable to replace the traditional secretary who types, transcribes, files, makes appointments, and coordinates meetings with the word processing operator who performs one specialized task? On the other hand, in some firms automation clearly has opened up opportunities for clerical workers to take on higher-level responsibilities. For example, in the insurance industry, a clerical worker may assume responsibilities previously performed by the insurance adjuster. In banking, it is not unusual for the clerical employee to work with databases and spreadsheets.

The ultimate factor in determining whether unions will be successful in organizing office workers is the control that employees will have over workplace technologies. Ultimately, will this control result in pay equity? Will it satisfy other demands for enhancing workers' rights in the workplace? Time will tell.

INTEGRATED OFFICE SYSTEMS

Business expansion, rising costs, intense competition, and increasing sophistication of technology make it imperative for management to seek ways of achieving maximum productivity from office systems now being utilized. People, procedures, space, and related office activities are being combined into information systems. The ability to integrate the separate and distinct applications of word processing; data processing; telecommunications, including electronic mail; records management, including electronic filing; and photocomposition to provide information on company operations and productivity to all levels of decision makers has been made possible through the minicomputer. The total integrated office system is the key to solving problems of business management, and the development of software programs that give word processors the capabilities once reserved for computers is just one example of maximum equipment utilization.

Distinctions between machines utilized in word processing and computers are slowly disappearing. For example, computers are components of word processing systems, and electronic typewriters have moved into the computer area. Tasks strictly a function of data processing are now found in word processing software programs, such as arithmetic computations. Communication capabilities have merged telecommunications with word processing.

As systems are integrated, problems arise which must be resolved, such as:

- *Organizational Structure.* The design must include growth factors, and decisions must be made to determine whether a centralized or decentralized system should be established.
- *Service Orientation.* Word processing departments are service-oriented and must serve users' needs; data processing de-

partments adhere to strict time schedules and do not usually communicate directly with users.
- *Human Factors.* Word processing is sensitive to the needs of users and human support in productivity. Word processing equipment has been designed to take into consideration the needs of the operator. Originally, implementation of data processing did not consider operators' needs.
- *Organizational Controls.* Who will be in charge? To whom will management report?

As we approach the close of the twentieth century, we will see even more extraordinary changes in office design and organization. Secretaries, clerks, supervisors, managers, executives, and accountants who are now working in offices abounding in paperwork may find themselves communicating on terminals from one office to another by electronic equipment. A telephone coupler may be the connecting device from terminals to computers to printers. How exciting to have a paperless office in which all personnel do their own "thing" via keyboards!

The person who is seriously interested in an office career must be aware of the combination of factors that make up the office environment now and what it will be in the very near future.

PROJECTIONS FOR 2000

By the year 2000, nearly 90 percent of all American workers will earn their livings in offices. Clerical workers make up the largest single category of white-collar workers. However, employment is affected by office automation. Projections by the U.S. Bureau of Labor Statistics indicate that employment in occupations that utilize the new information processing technology—computers to store information, to bill, to perform payroll functions, and to do other clerical calculations; dictation equipment to record the spoken word; electronic filing systems to store documents—will decrease for clerical workers such as data-entry keyers, except composers (16 percent); payroll clerks (12 percent), directory assistance operators (18 percent), typists and word processors (14 percent), and stenographers (28 percent). However, because of the increasing use of computers throughout the economy, the number of jobs for computer and peripheral equipment operators is expected to grow at a faster rate than the average for all occupations. Also, a larger projected growth pattern than the average for total employment is anticipated for industries that employ clerical workers such as hotel desk clerks and new account banking clerks. The need for receptionists and information clerks is expected to increase, perhaps due to the difficulty in automating their duties.

Overall, though, the employment demand is projected to increase significantly more slowly than the average for total employment from 1986 to the year 2000.

Between 1986 and 2000, clerical employment as a whole is projected to rise from 19.8 million to 22.1 million, or about 11 percent. This employment growth will occur in service-producing industries that are expanding at a much faster rate than the goods-producing industries. Employment in finance, insurance, and real estate firms that have large clerical staffs is expected to account for 8 percent of the growth in total employment, or 1.6 million jobs. Within this sector, banking and credit appear to be the two fastest-growing industries. There also will be many new jobs in wholesale and retail trade establishments, construction, and governmental agencies.

Most of the growth will occur among clerical workers and those in managerial and management-related occupations. Although the increase in clerical workers is expected to exceed that of managerial staff, the overall growth rate will be less than half of that for managers because of office automation in banking, credit, and insurance.

Although the government also will account for increased employment, it is important to note that there will be a loss of approximately 45,000 clerical jobs affecting mainly typists, stenographers, payroll and timekeeping clerks, and statistical clerks.

The following charts indicate the projected rate of growth from 1986 to the year 2000 for some clerical jobs and the projected decrease in employment for others.

The reasons for the high demand for skilled office workers are basic: the office worker is needed in every community, large or small, and in every type of activity; the population is growing; more information from more sources is being collected from more places; the government is requiring greater reporting; more complex business operations require more data inputs for decision making; and more diversification within companies requires more data compilations and more communications with branches in other sections of the country.

CHART 3
Projected Rate of Growth for Clerical Jobs
1986–2000

Job Title	Estimated Employment 1986	Projected Employment 2000	Percent Growth 1986–2000
Computer Operators and Peripheral Equipment Operators	46,000	70,000	51
Data-Entry Keyers, composing	29,000	43,000	51
File Clerks	242,000	274,000	13
General Office Clerks	2,361	2,824	20
Mail Clerks	136,000	145,000	6
Receptionist and Information Clerks	682,000	964,000	41
Secretaries	3,234	3,658	13
Telephone Operators	353,000	391,000	11

Projected Rate of Decrease for Clerical Jobs
1985–2000

Data-Entry Keyers, except composing	400,000	334,000	−16
Directory Assistance Operators	32,000	27,000	−18
Statistical Clerks	71,000	52,000	−26
Stenographers	178,000	128,000	−28
Typists and Word Processors	1,002,000	862,000	−14

Based on Bureau of Labor Statistics, September 1987.

All evidence points to the fact that some clerical employment categories are decreasing while others are still increasing, some at a slower rate than in the past. Also, the automation of office functions requires new skills and knowledge. To prepare for a secure future, workers must gain these new skills and knowledge, which are best achieved through education and training. There are many job opportunities for individuals who have a sound basic education and good technical skills, who are adaptable, and who are motivated and challenged to accept positions of high responsibility in automated offices.

EQUAL EMPLOYMENT OPPORTUNITIES

Former President Lyndon B. Johnson said: "You do not take a person who, for years, has been hobbled by chains and liberate him, bring him up to the starting line of a race and then say, 'You are free to compete with all the others,' and still justly believe that you have been completely fair."

After the Civil Rights Act of 1964—which outlawed discrimination on the basis of race, sex, national origin, or religion—many employers changed their employment practices to improve job opportunities for minorities and women. Policies were revised, affirmative action plans devised, training and educational programs developed, and testing programs designed in accordance with Equal Employment Opportunity (EEO) guidelines. Although women and minorities still do not have equal opportunities with the majority of men in all categories, nor always receive comparable earnings for similar responsibilities, management nevertheless has been forced to bring them into higher-level jobs.

This can best be illustrated by the following statistics on women workers taken from *Automation of America's Offices*. In 1983, women accounted for 80 percent of the administrative support workers and only 32 percent of the managers, administrators, and executives. When they achieve higher-level positions, they are mostly in the lower rungs of management.

Another example of inequality that supports the continued historical differences in the job market is reflected in the computer and technical specialist occupations where employment and opportunities are increasing. Women have been involved in the field from the beginning, and the growth of this industry occurred as affirmative action was implemented. Nevertheless, salaries for women at every level are less than those of their male counterparts.

Employment opportunities for minorities have improved during the last decade. This has resulted from a growing economy, affirmative action, and an active interest in social change in America. For minority women, the movement into clerical jobs represented an important means for upward social mobility. Black workers in 1985 accounted for 10.2 percent of the clerical work force, which is comparable to the black share of the labor force; and Hispanic Americans (includes black and white) accounted for 5 percent of this occupational category.

It is only within the last 30 years that black and Hispanic women have been able to move into office occupations. This has enabled many of them to move into the middle class. By 1980, approximately 29 percent of employed black women held clerical/administrative jobs and in 1987, 26 percent were in these positions. As the article "Office Work and Minorities" suggests, the difference might be attributable to the fact that as options opened up, educated black women may have moved out of clerical work into supervisory, management, and professional positions.

According to the 1985 statistics reported in *Women at Work,* approximately 28 percent of the Hispanic women in the work force held clerical positions compared to 30 percent of white women. Over 9 percent of the number of black men in the labor force were in administrative support/clerical positions, compared to 5.5 percent of white men.

The prospects look good for minorities for the next fifteen years. However, with the pattern of job growth in higher technology occupations and with the changing skills required for beginning and mid-level jobs—some with good potential for advancement—more education is required. Minority women will have to obtain more formalized and more off-the-job training to maintain the rate of progress they have made. A factor that might impede their opportunities is the movement of offices from cities to suburbs and the development of industries in the South and Southwest—areas with smaller minority populations.

The government, up to the present, has been a significant source of employment for minorities. However, this is likely to stabilize. In fact, as the figures show, employment has declined for certain occupations.

Many programs in private industry and in government have helped overcome barriers to employment for great numbers of minorities and disadvantaged workers. There also is pressure on business to hire disadvantaged youth. Through training and retraining programs, the federal government has made it possible for those who are unemployed or on the fringes of the labor force to become permanent, full-time workers. It has helped train those employed in low-income jobs to become more productive and successful, and it has discovered and will continue to ascertain the potential of those now considered unemployable.

Direct federal involvement in employment and training programs that were successful in promoting productive employment of jobless and underemployed youths and adults began with programs authorized by the Manpower Development and Training Act (MDTA) of 1962, the Economic Opportunity Act of 1964, and subsequent legislation—Job Opportunities in the Business Sector (JOBS), Neighborhood Youth Corps, Public Service Careers (PSC), Work Incentive Program (WIN), Institutional Training, Operation Mainstream, Jobs for Progress (SER) and Urban League on-the-job training.

In 1973 the Comprehensive Employment and Training Act (CETA) was passed. It was designed primarily to operate at the local level. In 1982, it was replaced in its entirety by the Job Training and Partnership Act (JTPA), which shifted its focus from income maintenance to training of unemployed, displaced workers. The purpose was to offer training in skills relevant to employment opportunities that existed. No longer was the federal government to be directly involved in training programs. Rather, a partnership was formed between private industry councils (PICs), local units of government, and educational program providers. The target groups included low-skilled adults, especially women and minorities; disadvantaged youth; and individuals residing in depressed areas.

Whereas the JTPA was industry-sponsored training, another

measure enacted in 1984 to improve public and vocational training was the Vocational Education Act, also known as the Perkins Act. Individuals that benefited from these programs were primarily the handicapped and disadvantaged, single parents and homemakers, and adults in need of training and retraining.

The success of these programs was based on adequate funding. According to *Automation of America's Offices,* however, federal funding decreased for employment and training by almost 50 percent between 1981 and 1984 and by 8.9 percent for elementary, secondary, and vocational education. In 1985, increases were extended in the amount of 14 percent for training and employment and 17.5 percent for education. Projections through 1990, however, indicate a decrease.

More recent proposals aimed at giving workers the opportunity to improve their skills, including those who are displaced by adverse economic conditions, include the following:

- Worker Readjustment Act, Title I-C, of the Trade, Employment and Productivity Act of 1987, which would replace Title III of the Job Training Partnership Act (JTPA) and the Trade Adjustment Assistance (TAA), a 1981 program that authorized funds for training. The services provided would include assessment, counseling, and job search assistance as well as retraining.
- AFDC and Summer Youth Employment and Training Amendments of 1987, Title I-D of the President's proposed Trade, Employment and Productivity Act of 1987, which would focus on the welfare youth population. The purpose is to break the cycle of welfare dependency by providing an enriched year-round program and to carry out the traditional summer youth program. Counseling, basic and remedial education, preemployment and work maturity skills, occupational training, employment experience, and support services would be provided in the program.
- Another program to eradicate welfare dependency is a private program for minority single female parents (MSFP) funded by the Rockefeller Foundation in 1981 and implemented by

Wider Opportunities for Women in Washington, D.C.; The Center for Employment Training in San Jose, California; the Urban League in Atlanta, Georgia, and several others. Significant funding was provided by the Women's Bureau of the Department of Labor to provide for child-care services. Interim findings focus on five central issues: parenting, basic skills, job training and placement, individualized support, and coordination of services in a single environment.

- The New York City Department of Employment (DOE) has developed a competency-based employment training program known as the Youth Pre-Employment/Work Maturity Competency System. Students receive instruction in all of the requisite skills necessary to find and be successful in a job, including good human relations skills. When ready for graduation from the program, students must demonstrate a mastery of the competencies taught.

Robert W. Stein, former manager of employee development for the Fisher Scientific Company in Pittsburgh, Pennsylvania, says with the authority based on his experience as a training and development specialist with several major companies, that the disadvantaged young woman or man considering clerical employment should do so optimistically, for:

"Applicants who can demonstrate that they have something to offer, something that will help in the achievement of organizational goals, will be interviewed and appraised more honestly now than ever before. This means that the individual contemplating clerical employment must make certain that he or she enters the job market with the proper skills, knowledge, and attitude not only to acquire a desirable position but to do well in this position once it has been secured. To the aspiring young person I would just like to say: Prepare yourself in these three areas, and I think you will find the road to success much less rocky than you anticipated."

CHANGES IN AGE AND GENDER OF CLERICAL WORKERS

The number of office jobs will continue to grow but at a slower pace. Probably, the lower-level routine jobs, such as data entry, will decline. It is estimated by the U.S. Bureau of Labor Statistics that although the population will grow by about 10 percent, the labor force will expand about 16 percent, from 113.5 million to well over 131 million. Of this number, about 65 percent of the new entrants in the work force will be women; and by 1995, they will make up approximately 47 percent of the work force. The number of working women aged 35 to 44 is expected to double, and there should be a 60 percent increase in the number of women between 45 and 55 years. As of spring 1987, more than one out of every ten workers in the United States was a women over the age of 55. Those who are already employed are mainly in clerical occupations.

The figures below show the continued growth rate of women in the labor force. In 1920, there were two women workers for every ten men workers. Today, more than four and one-half out of every ten American workers are women. (See Chart 4.) The period of the greatest growth for women was between 1960–1980. According to *Databook: Perspectives on Working Women,* the number of employed women during this time rose from 23.3 million to 44.1 million, a jump of 90 percent compared to a 29 percent rise for men, from 46.4 million to 59.8 million. (See Chart 5). By 1987, 50.5 million women and 63 million men were in the labor force.

Trends reflect that approximately 16 million middle-aged and older women will work outside the home. Contrary to myths that middle-aged and older women are stuck in their ways and resistant to change, studies show that older workers perform as well and perhaps better than younger workers. Also, as the rate of labor force participation for older men goes down and the rate for women increases, women will make more demands on employers and society. They will seek advancement, training opportunities, and provisions for child and dependent care.

Another important statistic concerning working women is that

**CHART 4
Increase in Women Workers in Total Labor Force
1920–1987**

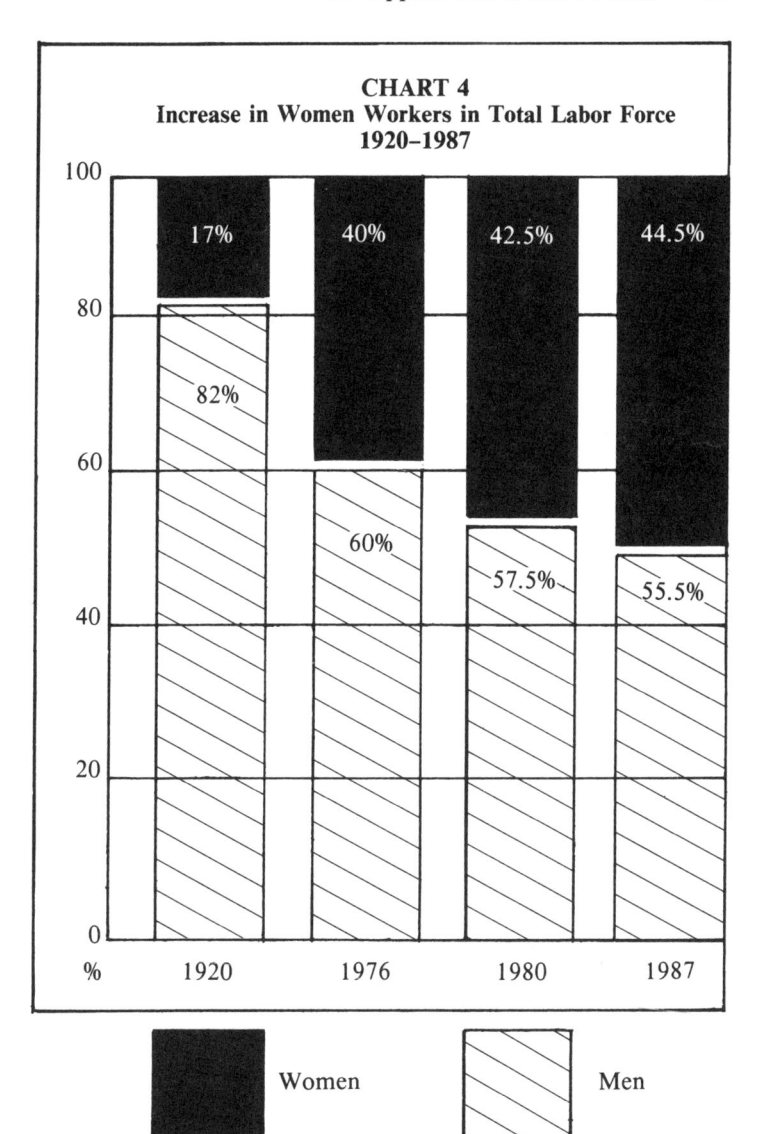

Year	Women	Men
1920	17%	82%
1976	40%	60%
1980	42.5%	57.5%
1987	44.5%	55.5%

CHART 5
**Increase in Number of Men and Women Employed in Labor Force
1960–1987**

*Based on data from U.S. Department of Labor

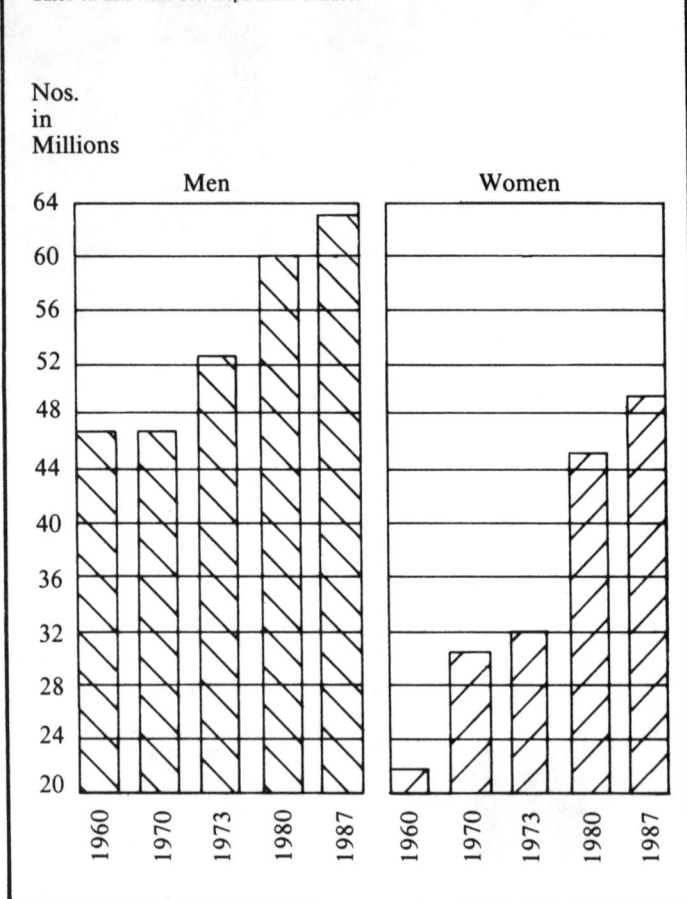

it is the norm for them to remain in the work force. As reported in "Working Mother is Now Norm," the 1987 data indicate that 50.8 percent of new mothers remained in the work force after giving birth. This marks the first time a majority of women reported they were working or actively seeking employment within a year of giving birth. Of those who remained in the job market, 68 percent were women who had their first child after 30 years of age, as against 54 percent of those women who had their first child between the ages of 18 and 24.

THE KINDS OF CLERICAL POSITIONS IN WHICH MEN OR WOMEN ARE STILL PREDOMINANT TODAY

It is not too surprising to find women in over nine-tenths of the receptionist or secretarial positions, but it is quite surprising to discover than even the bookkeeping positions, which have been traditionally held by men, are now more than nine-tenths filled by women. However, men still predominate in clerical positions in distribution, scheduling, and adjusting.

EMPLOYMENT PERSPECTIVES OF WORKING WOMEN

With so many women working in the administrative and clerical occupations categories (they constitute about 80 percent of all clerical workers), it is important that each woman views her needs for economic independence, particularly since she will probably work for approximately 25 years during her life. A look at figures compiled by the U.S. Bureau of Labor Statistics indicates a new mix of working women—a group of married, widowed, divorced, separated, or single women. Of approximately 50 million women in the labor force in the second quarter of 1987, 61 percent of them were married. In 1987, 52 percent of mothers with children one year and younger were in the labor force, and 60 percent had children between toddler age and first grade. Seventy-five percent of young women no longer in school were in the labor force. Understandably, employment participation rates of women who graduated from college were approximately 96 percent compared to 45 percent for those who dropped out of school.

CHART 6
Clerical Occupations in which 75 Percent or More of the Workers Are Women, 1985

Occupation	Percent
Bookkeepers	91.2
Data-Entry Keyers	91.3
Receptionists	96.9
Secretaries	98.3
Personnel Clerks, except Payroll and Timekeeping	90.6
Telephone Operators	92.8
Tellers	91.4
Typists	95.7
Billing Clerks	87.2
File Clerks	82.6
General Office Clerks	80.9
Payroll Clerks	81.4
Records Clerks	81.7
Information Clerks	88.9
Stenographers	86.6
Statistical Clerks	75.4

Many women in the 16- to 24-year old age group also work while attending school. Of the 17 million women in this age group, approximately 40 percent of high school youth, 50 percent of the full-time college students, and 90 percent of part-time students were in the labor force. Generally, these students need to work in occupations which offer flexibility in the workday. Therefore, they are typically employed in clerical, sales, or service jobs.

The most dramatic increase in labor force participation rates has been for Hispanic women, due to the high growth rate in population primarily from immigration. The number of employed Hispanics has risen more than half a million since 1986, which increased the rate of employment for Hispanics by 8 percent. Of this number, the sharpest rise was among Hispanic women. During 1987, 12 percent more women—300,000 additional Hispanic women—were in the labor force than the previous year. The employment of men in this group rose at only half that pace. In comparison to the rates for black and white women, the employment-population ratio for Hispanic women rose considerably higher.

In present-day society, the entire philosophy of women has changed. Women in the younger age bracket no longer enter the work force with the intention of staying only until they marry or have children. The mature woman who stayed home to raise a family first has either gone back to school to gain employable skills or has entered the labor market. Approximately two-thirds of all employed women work to support themselves and their families, or to help raise the families' standards of living.

Just what is the significance of these statements? It is apparent that the female labor force is significantly different from past decades. Even to the high school student not yet at work, they have meaning. In general, they say:

1. that there are now and probably will continue to be proportionately more jobs in the clerical field than in others;
2. that most clerical occupations are feminized, except for some key positions in data processing and office management;
3. that additional training will be needed to fill the new jobs brought about by automation;
4. that, as statistics indicate that work is today not merely a stopgap until marriage, management will give more consideration to additional training for women and there will be increasingly more opportunities for them to advance to higher positions;
5. that successful employees are those who are flexible and able to adapt to changes in the work environment—equipment, procedures, and workspace;
6. that ongoing education becomes more important as changes occur in employment opportunities;
7. that legislation enacted during the past decade barring discrimination in employment on the basis of sex should make available new opportunities for women, should enable them to secure more diversified jobs, and should enable them to

secure and advance to jobs requiring more responsibility and a higher skill level than was formerly possible;
8. that businesses are more cognizant of the needs of working mothers and are becoming more supportive in terms of child care and health centers.

EMPLOYMENT PROSPECTS FOR OLDER WORKERS

There has been a growing interest in older workers for several reasons: the serious labor shortage resulting from the declining birthrate in the 1960s and 1970s; the aging of the baby boom work force, those individuals born between 1945 and 1960; the rise of the service sector; technological change; and changing demands on social security, pension, and health systems. By the year 2000, over 60 million individuals (about 23 percent of the population) will be between the ages of 45 and 64. Shortly after 2000, the population of this age group will begin to decline; then the baby bust generation will enter this age range.

Bill Crawford reports in the *AARP News Bulletin* that Dr. Lydia Bronte of the Carnegie Corporation discerns a definite trend toward hiring persons in this category. She states that age 65 is no longer an indicator of old age and that "All these efforts [by corporations] to hire older people are worth pursuing because they often get an experienced, savvy, reliable worker who knows a specific field and environment. . . . Many companies are starting to realize it pays off in the long run to hire people with proven skills."

An AARP survey cites a study conducted by Yankelovich, Skelly and White, Incorporated, to determine employers' perceptions of older workers, which revealed that older workers are productive, reliable, committed to quality performance, and cost effective. The lowest ratings were received in adaptability to new technology, flexibility, and competitiveness.

Companies interested in attracting these experienced and mature workers are offering flexible work schedules, training, and higher-than-minimum wages. Some employers have even developed program options and work schedules for the individual who wants to work less than full-time. Some of these innovative programs and practices include job sharing and labor pools of retired personnel. A few of the companies reaching out to the older worker are The Travelers of Hartford, Connecticut; Grumman Aerospace in Los Angeles; Sterile Design Incorporated in Tampa, Florida; and the Los Angeles-based Aerospace Corporation.

CLASSIFICATION OF WORKERS IN THE CLERICAL OCCUPATIONS

People in offices who process papers or who handle related activities are classified as *clerical workers*. Depending on their duties, there are many kinds of clerical workers: general clerks, special clerks (such as mail, payroll, or file clerks), machine operators, bookkeepers, stenographers, secretaries, proofreaders, copy editors, and administrative support workers. In a small office, there may be only one general office worker who does all of the paperwork connected with the operation. One employer will call this worker "my clerk"; another will refer to the employee as "my secretary"; and a third may call this same person "my administrative assistant."

In larger offices, the duties become more specialized, and office management has been trying for years to develop titles that suggest specific duties and responsibilities so that everybody can understand what is meant by a particular job title. Job classification, though, is in its infancy. A person has only to read the "Help-Wanted" column to realize that one company may advertise for a "secretary," while another company will describe identical duties and ask for a "clerk."

The definitions of titles used in this book are taken from the government's attempt at standardization, *The Dictionary of Occupational Titles*. According to this source, an office clerk performs any combination of the following and similar clerical tasks in an office where typing is not required:

> "Copies information from one record to another. Sorts, files, and retrieves records or other documents. Addresses and stuffs envelopes. Sorts and distributes mail. Proofreads, records, and reports.

Duplicates records, using copying machine. Answers telephone and records or relays messages."

An administrative clerk (general office clerk) performs the following clerical duties, utilizing knowledge of systems or procedures:

"Copies data and compiles records and reports. Tabulates and posts data in record books. Computes wages, taxes, premiums, commissions, and payments. Records orders for merchandise or service. Gives information to and interviews customers, claimants, employees and sales personnel. Receives, counts, and pays out cash. Prepares, issues, and sends out receipts, bills, policies, invoices, statements, and checks. Prepares stock inventory. Adjusts complaints. Operates office machines, such as typewriter, adding, calculating, and duplicating machines. Opens and routes incoming mail, answers correspondence, and prepares outgoing mail. May take dictation. May prepare payroll. May keep books. May purchase supplies. May be designated according to field of activity or according to location of employment as Airport Clerk (air transportation); Death-Claim Clerk (insurance); Field Clerk (clerical); Colliery Clerk (mining and quarrying)."

In addition to general clerks with nonspecialized duties, there are highly specialized types of clerks who perform one routine duty at a high level of competency. For instance, a person who uses a calculator and typewriter to calculate and prepare customer invoices is classified as a billing clerk. A person who sorts incoming and outgoing mail all day long is classified as a distribution clerk. A clerk whose sole duty is to help travelers plan trips by responding to questions about time schedules, rates, and accommodations is a travel clerk. For practical purposes, the term clerk refers to one who performs office duties not generally assigned to bookkeepers, stenographers, salespeople, or managers.

The Administrative Management Society has prepared a condensed guide for twenty job classifications, entitled *Office Salaries Report,* that gives a quick overall picture of common types of clerical positions in offices throughout the United States and Canada.

A Word Processing Operator - Level B— Uses word processing equipment to input and edit typed documents with established quality and time standards. Equipment includes the tity. Obtains prices and specifications. Compiles records, such as items purchased or transferred between departments, prices, deliveries, and inventories. Confers with suppliers concerning late deliveries. May verify bills from suppliers with bids and purchase orders.

N Secretary - Level B— Performs a limited range of secretarial duties in a small company or for a supervisor in a larger firm. Duties may include taking dictation; transcribing from notes and/or dictation equipment; screening calls; making appointments; handling travel arrangements; answering routine correspondence; and maintaining filing systems.

O Secretary - Level A— Performs an unlimited range of secretarial duties for middle management personnel or more than one individual. Composes and/or takes and transcribes correspondence of a complex and confidential nature. Position requires a knowledge of company policy.

P Executive Secretary/Administrative Assistant— Performs a full range of secretarial and administrative duties for high-level member of executive staff. Handles project-oriented duties and may be held accountable for the timely completion of these tasks. Relieves executive of routine administrative detail. Position requires an in-depth knowledge of company practice and structure and a high degree of secretarial/administrative skills.

Q Legal Secretary/Assistant— Performs secretarial and/or administrative support services for a legal department or firm. Position requires some knowledge of legal terminology. May perform legal-related research activities; may utilize word processing or computer equipment.

R Switchboard Operator/Receptionist— Receives and directs incoming calls, greets visitors, performs basic clerical tasks.

S Clerk Typist— Produces draft and/or finished typed copies of documents from a variety of originators. Form and content usually follow standard guidelines. May perform other clerical duties of minimum difficulty.

T Customer Service Representative— Provides guidance and assistance to customers regarding problems with accounts or merchandise. Duties include searching records, investigating problems/complaints, policy interpretation, response preparation and adjustment, and correction of records.

CHAPTER 2

THE CLERK

The office environment has been affected by technological advances that change the way work is performed. Frequently, such a workplace is referred to as the "electronic office" or the "automated office." These designations simply imply that automated equipment is now being integrated into work processes and that changes in systems and procedures have been implemented.

Clerical workers are needed in every type of office—insurance, finance, banking, manufacturing, public utilities, medical, legal, advertising, publishing, and communications. They perform a wide variety of functions in the day-to-day operations of business and professional organizations; namely, process mail, operate equipment, handle the telephone, perform messenger duties, and act as receptionists. Some may work as assignment clerks, file clerks, bank tellers, invoicing-systems operators, or equipment operators.

The skill, education, and training for success in a clerical work environment vary with the type of job. There are more clerks in business occupations than any other category of worker below the management level.

Clerical work carries the lowest classification among the office positions. It ranks lowest in the salary scale, and it requires less specialized job preparation than any other office position. On the other hand, it is the most common job for which the beginning worker is hired, and it is often used as the job station in which a new employee learns the work of the office. Although office technology has created new job opportunities, it is important to realize that jobs are declining for those who have limited training and who are able to perform only simple, routine tasks. Basic to job success in most clerical positions is a knowledge of keyboarding, business English, office procedures, and human relations skills. Equally important are good attitudes: cooperativeness, dependability, honesty, and responsibility.

A few years ago, the usual practice in business was to hire superior academically prepared graduates for clerical work and train them on the job. This procedure, however, cost the employer too much money, for the employees often found that, after trying clerical work at company expense, they were not suited to routine work and soon resigned. Business today is more likely to look to the high schools for its clerks, who have been trained at public expense. These graduates become productive workers much sooner, do not object to the routine work involved, and are willing to stay on their jobs.

Most of the large firms in the United States provide some type of on-the-job training or orientation programs for their new employees and retraining for the relocation of their older employees. Progressive companies recognize that training on the job leads to work satisfaction and personal fulfillment, thus making an employee more valuable.

Though clerical work is often rather routine, there are varied types of clerical jobs which may appeal to different interests and abilities. In addition to general clerks, who may perform tasks of a varying nature, there are such specialized clerks as file clerks, receptionists and information clerks, data-entry clerks, billing clerks, electronic typesetting machine operators, and computer-output-microfiche operators. The jobs at the bottom of the skill ladder are diminishing, and there is an increasing need for employees with basic skills and specialization because of office automation.

CHANGING ACTIVITIES OF THE CLERK

Today's office is in a state of change, which is reflected in the way certain tasks are performed. However, the office still functions as the nerve center of management—the brain of the business organization. This nerve center, which is composed of clerical workers, must function efficiently and speedily. Many of the detailed and repetitive tasks have been automated, and the work performed is more sophisticated than it was.

Some of the responsibilities of the clerk are listed below. They are not arranged in order of importance or frequency.

- Maintaining a mail register
- Preparing a digest of incoming mail
- Sorting, opening, dating, routing, and distributing mail
- Handling the telephone and telephone systems
- Using telephone directories
- Being aware of the latest telephone equipment and being able to relate need to executives
- Using the variety of telephone services available
- Being able to organize a teleconference call
- Keeping payroll records
- Keeping a petty cash fund and administering it
- Preparing cash and checks for deposit
- Preparing a deposit slip
- Preparing, endorsing, and stopping payment on checks
- Reconciling a bank statement
- Completing purchase requisition forms
- Ordering by telephone
- Choosing a reprographics process
- Duplicating or copying information
- Preparing and paying vouchers
- Handling and sorting source documents, such as requisitions, bills, payment checks, notices, and adjustments
- Filling in printed forms on the typewriter
- Copying from rough draft or corrected copy on the typewriter
- Receiving callers

- Cataloging addresses, prices, and other data
- Typing numeric data
- Writing numeric data
- Proofreading numeric data
- Duplicating or copying information (Xerox and offset machines)
- Using the calculating machine, particularly the ten-key electronic calculator
- Detecting errors
- Handling printed reports
- Recording data in handwritten form
- Keying in data to typewriters, cash registers, calculators, keypunch machines, and key-to-tape machines to get printouts
- Verifying or listing information about business papers
- Coding information
- Classifying, storing, updating, and retrieving office information
- Readying data to be converted to machine-reading language
- Microfilming
- Using indexing systems for mechanized storage
- Retrieving data from microfilm, magnetic tapes, and documents
- Composing and typing letters
- Reviewing machine outputs
- Amending corrected data and entering them properly into the system
- Keyboarding
- Transcribing from machine dictation
- Performing research
- Communicating orally
- Taking inventory
- Operating other office machines and managing records

COMPUTERIZATION IN THE OFFICE

The changes that have resulted from computers appearing on desktops have affected personnel ranging from clerical all the way up to top-level management. This has presented a challenge to learn new skills and procedures not only for administrative support employees but also for managers. Most important is that administrators learn every aspect of the equipment and its capabilities in order to apply the new technology to the needs of the organization. A look at a few business and professional offices reveals the following:

Legal Firms. In "Is the Computer Fostering a More Just Justice System?," Susan Kerr cites a 1987 survey of 500 law firms in the nation that reported that 13 percent of the lawyers had computers on or near their desks, a jump from 7 percent in 1986. Of the total number of users, 38 percent were litigation specialists and 26 percent were corporate law specialists, followed by tax, real estate, and trust/estate attorneys. The computer is used mainly for word processing and legal research. Those lawyers who operate the computer learned to use it independently.

Approximately 70 percent of the secretaries in the firms surveyed use word processing, a 22 percent increase from 1986. This did lead to staff reduction, however, in 40 percent of the firms.

The courts are using computers to track cases and schedule court sessions. Computerized court transcription systems are being developed, and it is not uncommon for court reporters to provide lawyers with floppy disks rather than typed transcripts. Putting legal court records on magnetic media is the wave of the future.

Banks. Banks are probably one of the biggest users of automated equipment. They are looking forward to the day when all checks will be handled electronically when they enter the bank. The increased use of automatic teller machines and electronic funds transfer has resulted in a slowdown in the employment growth of bank tellers. However, they still account for almost 23 percent of total employment. Their productivity has risen 20 percent because of the online terminals. Now they can post customer transactions or respond to customer requests for bank balances in a few seconds. In general, clerical employment grew at a much faster pace than the average growth rate for other types of work. However, according to a study by Matthew Drennan, cited in "Office Automation" by William M. Austin and Lawrence C. Drake, Jr., that trend will reverse itself after 1990.

In commercial banking, clerical occupations constitute the largest occupational group; and the number is expected to increase through 1995. While clerks involved with financial records and information clerks who handle new accounts, traveler's check issuance, and general information will increase, the number of file clerks is expected to decline slightly.

Credit Agencies. In credit agencies, excluding banks, the following types of workers constituted over 44 percent of the total industry employment: tellers, loan and credit clerks; financial managers; general office clerks; and bookkeeping, accounting, and auditing clerks.

Security and Commodity Brokers and Investment Services. In addition to sales agents who accounted for 28 percent of the industry employment, clerical staff—including brokerage clerks, secretaries, and general office clerks—made up approximately 27 percent of the labor force.

Insurance. Clerical workers made up 53 percent of the total employment in the insurance carriers industry.

Real Estate. The clerical employees numbered 22.3 percent of the industry employment. A look at a combined total for real estate, insurance, loan, and law offices reflects that clerical workers accounted for an average of 37.7 percent of the work force.

Health Care. The demand for qualified medical assistants is rising, and the U.S. Bureau of Labor Statistics predicts about a 53 percent increase in the number of assistants needed through 1995.

WHAT SKILLS ARE IMPORTANT?

The new technology not only affects employment opportunities and the structure of work but also the job responsibilities of office personnel. Clerical workers are no longer just cogs in the wheels; rather, the jobs they perform are pertinent to the overall goals of businesses. They must, therefore, be aware of the total business operation and must assume a sense of responsibility in their work. Concomitant with this obligation are good attitudes and the necessity for promptness, for accuracy, for meeting deadlines, for follow-up, for initiative, for wise judgment, and for decision making.

Clerical workers must have the basic skills of reading, writing, and calculating. They must be able to write grammatically and punctuate and spell correctly. Very important is the skill of listening to and carrying out instructions, the ability to communicate orally via the telephone and in person, and the facility and personality to get along with people, both inside and outside the company. A good clerical worker must also be able to accept and act upon valid criticism.

Every clerical job involves typewriting, and the typist's job itself has become more sophisticated, requiring more background in business and more independent judgment. Also, those who aspire to clerical positions should be able to operate numerous other office machines and to file business papers. Considerable effort has been made to establish standards of performance in the commonest clerical jobs. In general, it can be said that a clerk should be able to:

- Type at least 55 words per minute;
- File cards or remove them from the files at the rate of 300 per hour;
- Retrieve from files 30 letters in 20 minutes;
- Fill in 100–150 addresses on form letters by typewriter in an hour.

In "Clerical Competencies for the Automated Office of the Future," Richard C. Erickson and Yves A. Asselin report the findings of a study conducted to identify and prioritize competencies required by clerical personnel. The competencies were clustered under six groups: language and communication skills, attitudes and personal traits, equipment-related skills, management skills, numerical and recordkeeping abilities, and understanding concepts and processes.

The conclusions indicated that communication and language skills, attitudes, personal traits, equipment-related skills, time management, work organization, decision making, problem solving, file-

56   *Opportunities in Office Occupations*

related tasks, and office automation concepts and terminology are high priority competencies for clerical workers. More specifically, under each of the five categories used in the study, the following competencies, traits, and attitudes were deemed to be very important.

Language and Communication

- Use of good listening skills
- Application of correct English usage
- Selection of appropriate information for report preparation
- Format documents
- Edit documents
- Screen phone calls

Attitudes and Personal Traits

- Use of discretion in confidential matters
- Interest in work
- Acceptance of responsibility
- Flexible
- Versatile
- Leadership qualities
- Innovative and creative
- Acceptance of constructive criticism
- Follow oral and written instructions
- Work under pressure
- Honest and loyal
- Work effectively with people
- Cooperative
- Receive visitors politely
- Accept challenges presented by new office equipment and procedures
- Exhibit good human relations skills
- Exercise good judgment
- Ability to operate word and data processing equipment, electromagnetic storage devices, and microcomputers

Management Skills

- Set priorities

- Organize office work

Numerical and Recordkeeping

- Maintain a filing system
- Develop, process, and maintain electronic files
- Store information on electronic devices
- Process messages with electronic mail

Concepts and Processes

- Comprehend concepts and terminology on automation
- Understand role played by computers and telecommunications systems in processing information
- Know capabilities and limitations of microcomputers

EDUCATIONAL PREPARATION

In most companies, high school graduation is the minimum educational requirement for employment in clerical work. Usually, the employer also wants specialized training for office work; and many high schools have developed clerical curricula to prepare graduates for those office duties not generally assigned to bookkeepers, secretaries, salespeople, or managers. The business subjects usually included, and those that will be vocationally most useful to clerical support staff are: keyboarding, bookkeeping/accounting or recordkeeping, office procedures or office technology, introduction to occupations, economics of work, data processing/computer applications, personal resource management, and duties of the office assistant.

Students from schools offering only general education components have the option of attending an area vocational school for training. Noteworthy is a unique program offered by the Office Occupations Divisions in the 916 area vocational technical institutes in Minnesota that teaches students the skills required for specialized office employment. The twelve curricula offered in this program qualify graduates as: timekeepers, accounts receivable clerks, records management clerks, policy typists, claims clerks, records clerks, raters, policy analysts and interpreters, expeditors, dispatchers, and tracing clerks. This training prepares students for work in a variety of offices (educational, banking and finance, accounting, traffic, purchasing, law enforcement, insurance, and medical data processing) and is coordinated with the high school districts from which students are transported for two hours of classes each day.

Units of work that usually are included in an office procedures course focus on the telephone, interpersonal skills/human relations, information technology, business filing and records control, clerical applications of keyboarding (filling in forms, preparing copy for duplicating, keyboarding from rough draft), telecommunications technology, reprographics, and job searching and career planning. The classrooms are sometimes organized like real offices to help students learn the interrelationships of different office jobs. In some schools, a new technique called "cooperative learning" is being used to motivate and help students learn. Students work in groups and coach one another.

In addition to classroom experiences, students have many other opportunities to learn about office work. One of these is the school business club, which may invite alumni who are business leaders to describe their jobs. The club may sponsor field trips to offices in the neighborhood or arrange other activities to bring business nearer the classroom. Another good learning experience is summer or after-school work in an office. Although the positions for which students can qualify involve primarily routine work, they nevertheless offer plenty of opportunities to learn about office procedures and how to get along with fellow workers. Another way to get some office experience prior to graduation from high school is to work in your school's office. Sometimes this work is assigned as part of a clerical practice course.

Many high schools have a cooperative work-study program. Students go to school half-time and work in offices for pay the other half. They may go to school in the morning and work in the afternoon or go to school and to the office on alternate weeks. A coordinator from the high school supervises the office work and arranges for school training in areas in which the student is deficient.

Another valuable learning experience is to "shadow" for one or two days a clerical support staff member of a firm. The student observes the daily routines and records the tasks performed. This is a realistic educational experience that is combined with classroom learning, for it bridges the gap between theory and practice.

COMMUNITY COLLEGES

Although clerical workers in past decades usually were trained in high schools, the community college, which had its greatest impetus in vocational education offerings during the 1960s and 1970s, has become an integral part of the American educational system. In these postsecondary institutions, students from diverse backgrounds may receive career training for specific occupations. Typical business programs offered at the community college level are accounting, word/information processing, marketing and management, business administration, records management, office technology, secretarial studies/office administration, and data processing/computer systems.

A look at figures from the 1987 *Statistical Abstract of the United States* in the technical/sales/administrative occupations shows that in 1986 a considerably higher percentage of females completed high school than males, 54.1 percent compared to 35 percent, respectively. Approximately the same number of females and males completed one to three years of college (26 percent), and considerably more males completed four years of college in this occupational category (31 percent compared to 13 percent).

College enrollments in both the public and private sectors are showing a decline. In 1982, over nine and one-half million students were enrolled in public schools and over two and one-half million in private schools. By 1993, projections indicate an enrollment of nine million in the public colleges and almost two and one-half million in the private institutions. The percentage of students who earned degrees below the bachelor's level in secretarial studies in 1982 was 32 percent, of which over 98 percent were female; in data processing, 27 percent earned similar degrees, of which 52 percent were female, according to the 1987 *Abstract.*

During the second half of the 1980s, community colleges have been experiencing a decrease in enrollment because of fewer high school graduates resulting from the drop in the birthrate during the 1960s and early 1970s. The population of 18- to 24-year-olds is anticipated to begin rising in the 1990s. To survive, colleges are responding by reaching out to other groups of potential students; namely, the reentry adult student, the worker under company tuition-reimbursement plans, the disadvantaged in need of remediation programs, foreign students, part-time students, and employees seeking education at off-campus sites near places of employment. Other means that have been used to lure students to enroll in college include giving credit for life experiences and providing advanced placement in specific courses.

Many colleges are also developing matriculation agreements with private business schools, which is another way to attract students to pursue their education after completing their course of study. Another route community colleges are pursuing to enhance their programs and to recruit students is to design technical programs that lead to a degree or certificate, such as in aviation technology, air-conditioning and refrigeration, and hotel and restaurant management.

Another group that needs to be addressed by community colleges is that comprising individuals working in small businesses in the immediate neighborhoods. Special courses, for example, in real estate, insurance, and travel need to be developed so that people can learn skills that will make them employable.

The New York City partnership's summer jobs program has helped 180,000 young people between 16 and 21 get jobs since 1981. The program matches these youth with businesses that provide challenging positions. In her article "Lena Horne Knows Well the Importance of 1st Job," Estelle Lander reports that in 1987, over 40,000 individuals from low-income families earned a combined 34 millions dollars.

It is important to recognize that community colleges offer students diverse career and education options. Since their basic philosophy is to meet the needs of the community, these colleges quickly revise, expand, and develop programs to meet changing employment situations and student interests.

Private business schools are also developing cooperative programs with firms, especially for such specialized clerical occupations as those needed in travel and tourism, marketing, and account management. Also, some businesses are sending their untrained clerks to private business schools for supplementary training on a part-time basis during their working hours.

COMPANY TRAINING

One need only check catalogs of colleges and universities to learn that many of these institutions are offering corporate training programs. This is in response to the increasing role that American business has begun to play in education. Initially, corporations began entering the education arena to close the gap that they believed existed between the needs of the workplace and what the schools were offering. As new technology was, is, and continues to be introduced into the work environment, companies need to provide training for their employees, training that meets their specific needs. In "The Trend to Electronic Training," Walter A. Kleinschrod argues that this type of training needs to be available to the following groups of individuals:

- Employees who are confronted with a microcomputer and the accompanying software for the first time (Statistics reflect that approximately one and one-half million workers get new microcomputers each month);
- Experienced users who receive new equipment or upgraded software;
- So-called newly hired "skilled" workers who need training in the procedures of the employing organization;
- Employees whose job responsibilities change and thus forget certain routines on equipment;
- Employees who perform jobs for end users and who consequently require knowledge of specialized software, such as spreadsheets and database management.

A 1986 Omni Group Limited survey of firms in New York City, cited by Kleinschrod, sought to determine how extensive was their training of personnel in computer skills. The survey indicated that

86 percent of the firms offered computer skills training; projections indicated that by 1988, 93 percent would have such programs. Almost 45 percent of these individuals were trained in classrooms; 29 percent were self-trained, using vendor manuals; and 8 percent used computer-assisted instruction.

Business itself provides three basic types of educational programs:

- *On-the-job training,* wherein the beginning worker is trained at his or her assigned job under the supervision of an experienced worker, often assisted by company manuals;
- *Vestibule training,* (usually conducted by larger firms) given away from the work area but during working hours, usually in an on-site classroom, using the same equipment, materials, and procedures as the actual job. (This training hopefully will raise the employee's level of skill, will orient him or her to company procedures, and will teach new skills to old employees, enabling them to qualify for promotion);
- *After-hours or off-premises training,* a volunteer program to improve skills to qualify for promotion, or to improve personal development.

The McGraw-Hill Book Company, Incorporated, has a one-week training program for its new employees before assigning them to a job. It also provides a continuing education program with courses designed to help employees gain additional skills and knowledge and to offer opportunities for professional growth. The Chase development center of the Chase Manhattan Bank also offers a range of courses from orientation programs for new employees to advanced professional training. The Eastman-Kodak Company's (Rochester, New York) education programs provide diverse courses for Kodak personnel who want to improve their job and communication skills. Instruction ranges from the fundamentals of reading and writing to computer programming. Many large corporations such as Merrill Lynch Pierce Fenner & Smith customize training programs to meet the current needs of their employees. Through personnel performance evaluations and needs assessments of the different departments, courses are designed to train and/or upgrade employees' communication, equipment, software, and systems' operational skills.

EDUCATIONAL INSTITUTIONS AND CORPORATE PARTNERSHIPS

This new relationship between education and the economy will contribute to the development of the nation's work force. In "Partnerships that Help the Economy," Robert Nielson argues that "The tendency in most 'partnerships for economic development' is to focus on a specific company's immediate technical job-training requirements."

Worth noting is the adopt-a-school program practiced by businesses throughout the nation. These are decentralized programs between individual schools and companies that are based on local needs and resources. To cite a few: in New York City, the Chase Manhattan Bank adopted Murray Bergtraum High School for Business Careers; Federal Express adopted Booker T. Washington High School in Memphis, Tennessee; Frito-Lay Corporation adopted Dallas's Caillet Elementary School, and American Can Company adopted Martin Luther King Junior High School. In New York City alone, half of the 110 high schools have some type of alliance with corporations and business groups. Some companies provide equipment, some focus on students, and others try to improve teacher training. Fairchild Industries, for example, pays teachers to become part-time summer employees and pays its own employees to become part-time teachers.

ABILITIES REQUIRED IN TOMORROW'S OFFICES

Office procedures are affected by technological advances. Office workers who advance beyond their entry-level jobs and who are involved in the processing of data and information need an overall understanding of how a business operates. They must be able to respond to the new methods of collecting, processing, storing, and retrieving information.

A review of the *1987 Model Curriculum Guides for Business Ed-*

ucation by the National Business Education Association emphasizes the basic skills and core competencies—including technical, personal, and conceptual abilities—that are needed now and in the future by all levels of clerical workers. These skills and competencies are:

- Information skills: reading, writing, speaking, listening, and computing;
- Personal development skills: self-management, interpersonal relations, decision making/critical thinking, leadership, and career awareness/goal setting;
- Economic, consumer, and business concept skills: American economic system, money management, and business and its environment;
- Technology skills: computer literacy and keyboarding.

More specifically, some of these competencies include:

- Ability to follow directions and to complete an application form;
- Ability to use correct punctuation, spell correctly, and write coherently using correct English usage;
- Ability to use reference materials;
- Ability to communicate orally and in writing, to give clear directions, to express oneself clearly and concisely in writing, to listen actively, to critique a presentation, and to read and understand;
- Ability to interpret numerical information and use computational skills;
- Ability to set personal goals, establish deadlines, and manage one's personal resources;
- Ability to work with others and to be cooperative, tactful, fair, courteous, and dependable;
- Ability to work using appropriate work attitudes: adaptability, punctuality, reliability, orderliness, trustworthiness, and integrity;
- Ability to make decisions and constructively evaluate situations;
- Ability to use critical thinking skills using inductive and deductive reasoning in problem solving;
- Ability to set priorities;

The Clerk 65

- Ability to use initiative and imagination, to motivate people, to develop confidence, and to delegate responsibility;
- Ability to reconcile a bank statement, prepare a personal budget, and understand a business organization from an economic, legal, and social point of view;
- Ability to use a microcomputer, to understand the steps in the processing cycle, to understand the ways in which a computer can be used in business and the effect of computers on consumers;
- Ability to keyboard, proofread, and compose at the machine.

The previously mentioned basic competencies that every individual should possess to keep pace with electronic advancements need to be elaborated upon in terms of office employment and promotion opportunities. The following skills can be added to the list given above:

- Ability to keyboard and transcribe speedily to achieve high levels of productivity;
- Ability to operate Telex/teletype machines, terminals, input and output devices, and central processing units;
- Ability to adjust to changing environments, procedures, and work sequences brought about by technology and the need for quick turnaround time;
- Ability to understand the flow of work in an organization, the functions of an office, the physical needs of employees regarding space allocations, prioritization, management of time, and logging information;
- Ability to prepare input media for automated processing, to understand word processing and data processing equipment, telecommunications, and reprographics;
- Ability to code documents and store, retrieve, use, protect, and transfer records; to apply micrographics to information storage and retrieval systems; and to develop and maintain records-management programs;

66   *Opportunities in Office Occupations*

- Ability to plan systems, set standards of performance; motivate, prepare, and control operating budgets; manage mail and messenger services, understand work objectives, and train personnel in system operations and routines;
- Ability to supervise employees, develop growth potential of personnel, provide job enrichment, and maintain personnel files and salary information;
- Ability to plan, coordinate, analyze, and report workloads and productivity;
- Ability to plan and design office space and to evaluate and select office furniture and equipment;
- Ability to make decisions, interpret numerical information, and use computational skills.

Perhaps this list exaggerates the requirements for an initial job, but it certainly indicates the directions the worker must take for promotion.

BEGINNING THE SEARCH FOR A JOB

Searching for a job can be tedious and at times depressing. However, candidates learn from each contact and personal interview. How do you get started? Experience has shown that the best means of finding out about job opportunities are the following: direct application to personnel departments, local newspaper help-wanted ads, school placement offices, private and state employment agencies, and referrals by friends and relatives. Be aggressive and explore every possibility, including teachers and the civil service. Below is a discussion on some of these approaches.

Businesses often seek office employees through school placement offices. That is one reason why good personality ratings in school and the attainment of high grades and specific skills are important. Too often, graduates bypass the placement office and try to get their jobs unaided, despite the fact that the office is there to assist them. Get acquainted with your placement office director, whose job it is to help graduates by matching job openings with qualified candidates. It is your responsibility to complete the necessary forms for registration and to report to the office regularly.

Information about job leads may come through friends or relatives. Many companies regard their present employees as their best recruiters of new workers. To follow such a lead is an accepted practice, but it is only the initial contact. From there on the qualifications of the applicants are the determining factors in their getting the job.

An excellent job can sometimes be obtained by applying at a private employment agency. The agency will have job candidates fill out application forms and, after assessing their skills, may send them on several interviews. Many companies like to hire people directly from employment agencies, since the agencies first screen all applicants and send only those who seem to fit the qualifications. A disadvantage is the fact that a private employment agency charges a fee for its services, usually a percentage of one month's salary. Fees vary from state to state. In New York State, the maximum is 60 percent. However, it is becoming a common practice for the employer to pay the fee.

Many people prefer to use the facilities of the local office of the state employment service. Representatives of these offices very often visit high schools near graduation to explain to the seniors how to register for a position. The location of the state employment service office is easily determined through the local telephone directory; its services are entirely free. In New York State, for example, joint programs are conducted with more than 700 high schools to provide counseling, aptitude testing, and placement for seniors about to enter the labor market. The service is anxious to help employers find qualified workers and to help workers find the most advantageous jobs for which they qualify.

Positions for clerks often are listed in the classified section of the newspaper. There are two kinds of want-ads—blind advertisements, requiring a letter of application, and complete advertisements, giving information that enables the applicant to arrange a personal interview at once. A blind advertisement describes the position but does not identify the employer. The applicant must address a letter of application to a box number; if the letter creates interest, the candidate gets the interview. In the recommended reading list at the end of this book, you will find excellent sources of information about how to write letters of application. You should study these carefully before preparing your own application letter.

Read newspaper ads carefully and do not be misled by phrases such as "opportunity of a lifetime" or "varied, interesting travel." What do these phrases mean? What is the job about? What is the starting salary? What are the chances for advancement?

Because matching people with the right jobs is so important, companies have central personnel departments where all applicants for positions are screened by trained interviewers. Candidates go to the personnel office for their first interviews and usually have conversations with members of the department, who form general impressions of the applicants' personal appearance, grooming, speech, and poise. The discussions, which usually revolve around candidates' interests and training, give the applicants an opportunity to demonstrate their understanding of the job requirements and to indicate how their qualifications meet those requirements.

Applicants are asked to complete application forms. Since much of clerical work involves understanding and following instructions, applicants should be most careful to complete the forms exactly as they are told. If the last name should be written first, an application from *Ann Roberts* instead of *Roberts, Ann* will get little attention.

EMPLOYMENT TESTING

The interview often is followed by a clerical test, or a battery of tests, which examines the clerical abilities of the applicants: filing, mathematical reasoning, spelling, grammar, proofreading. A widely used clerical test requires that the applicant recognize the similarity or dissimilarity of figures or names. For instance, the testee is asked to check only the pairs of names or numbers that are alike in a list such as:

1240459—1240459
2220459—2202459
John Anderson—John Andersen
Louis Rodriguez—Louis Rodriguez

Applicants for positions as clerks may also be asked to take a typewriting test. The usual straight-copy test is most often used, but the test may also include preparing a form letter from information given out of context or arranging material properly.

With the advent of automated equipment, it became necessary to measure an individual's ability to use electronic equipment. If the testing site is equipped with computers, then document formatting and the application of language skills can be tested right on the machine. However, budgetary constraints often prohibit the purchase of equipment for this purpose. Therefore, to test for knowledge of electronic equipment and operations, applicants can be asked questions about brand names of equipment and about specific function keys, commands, and procedures that are used to format documents. Applicants also can be asked to produce on an electronic typewriter a letter or report from unarranged copy. After completing the task, the applicant would need to indicate in the margin the command to be used to format the different sections of the report, if neither a word processor nor a microcomputer with software was available. For example, if the spacing varied from single to double to triple spacing or if there was indented material, the candidate would have to indicate the function key and procedure used to automatize the operation.

In summary, employment tests cover language skills, following directions, formatting documents correctly from unarranged copy, and the operation of word processing equipment or a microcomputer with word processing software. Less commonly, the applicant's knowledge of spreadsheets and databases is tested.

After approval by the personnel department, an applicant usually is sent directly to the department in which the vacancy exists for an interview with the supervisor. During this interview, the supervisor discusses the exact nature of the job and also has an opportunity to decide whether the prospective clerk will fit into that particular office and work well with the other clerks already there.

THE WORKING SITUATION

Many people prefer to enter white-collar jobs in offices rather than seek factory jobs because of the generally good working conditions most clerical employees enjoy. Also, most office workers get longer vacation periods than do blue-collar employees, and their working hours usually are shorter. In many firms, the work shift for clerical workers is being reduced to a 35-hour, four-day week. Some forecasters predict that by 1995 many employees will be working a 32-hour week. This is especially likely in companies that have expensive electronic equipment that must be operated on a twenty-four hour basis. Reports indicate that employees find this schedule convenient because they have more free time; management likes it because there is less absenteeism and greater productivity. Another attractive work concept to employees is flextime.

Office employees of large companies also receive many fringe benefits in addition to salary—benefits ranging from medical and hospital care, insurance, retirement pensions, paid vacations, and free lunches, to the privilege of buying stock in the company at reduced quotations.

A clerk's job, involving as it does many diversified duties, usually provides opportunities for development and promotion if the ability is there. These opportunities come through the trained supervision that is usually available and often may be supplemented by additional training at company expense. Clerks may specialize in routines that they like and for which they are well suited, eventually becoming accounting clerks, credit clerks, data-entry clerks, or file clerks. For a person looking for stability and a position that does not require aggressiveness or heavy responsibility, that of specialized clerk is appealing.

Automation has, no doubt, made some changes in the type of work done by clerical employees, but most experts agree that it has not decreased the number of clerical positions. Clerical workers in many offices now use electronic typewriters that have many automatic features, making original keyboarding and editing tasks much easier. Filing continues to be an important part of a clerk's job, but the materials being filed now include such items as microfiche and recorded disks instead of the usual papers. The ability of the clerk to work accurately—to read and follow instructions—will become increasingly important. The upgraded clerical jobs that are appearing in automated offices may necessitate increased training and higher native ability for clerical workers.

A clerical job provides more regularity of employment than factory work, which is affected by seasonal variations and by supply and demand. The clerk who performs the designated duties satisfactorily can usually count on stability of employment and regular advancement.

ALTERNATIVE WORK PATTERNS IN A TECHNOLOGICAL SOCIETY

The alternatives to the standard workday are temporary, part-time, contractual, flextime, and job-sharing employment. Both employees and employers derive many benefits from such work patterns. Individuals who have parenting responsibilities, who are enrolled in school, who have community responsibilities, or who are starting a small business require flexible, part-time, or temporary schedules. For people who like new faces and places, a temporary work-style is attractive. Other reasons for opting for temporary employment are to brush up on skills after returning to the labor market and to explore different types of companies and career possibilities. From an employer's viewpoint, these individuals are an excellent source of labor, particularly in times when a skilled labor shortage apparently exists. Another reason employers are using these approaches is to control costs.

Temporary Work. Temporary work, the third fastest growing industry, and increasing at a rate of 20 percent annually, is a viable career approach for millions of workers. Currently, more than 700,000 temporary jobs are filled each week, 60 percent of which are clerical. This industry is growing faster than the computer industry itself. Although opportunities are available for a varied work force, including file clerks, sales clerks, accountants, and operators of equipment, those individuals in greatest demand are secretaries, receptionists, word processors, and typists. There is also a growing need in this industry for programmers, systems analysts, data communications specialists, data processors, and medical technicians. In 1986, according to the National Association of Temporary Services (NATS), over five million temporary workers were employed.

No longer are temporaries just fill-ins for sick or vacationing employees. Companies now staff themselves for a minimum rather than a maximum work flow and use temporary help for additional tasks as they arise or for once-a-year, large-scale jobs.

The temporary worker is employed by the agency, and the agency receives its compensation from its client who uses its personnel. Time periods for jobs vary from a day to a year or more. Firms like Manpower, Olsten, Kelly Services, and Associated Staffing may be able to contract for special requests for work schedules. Many of them have also developed their own training programs that are particularly helpful to those individuals who do not know how to operate a computer or word processor. Generally, individuals with these skills are paid more per hour than are others for similar full-time jobs.

What does this burgeoning market mean to the persons interested in this pattern of employment? They should be willing to learn new skills, be flexible, have initiative, and be prepared to work independently.

Part-Time Work. An employee who works less than 35 hours a week is considered a part-time worker by the U.S. Bureau of Labor Statistics. Generally, part-time workers do not want to be tied down to a full-time job. With time, office automation will probably stimulate a continuing trend toward the use of part-time workers, as well as temporary workers. For many compelling reasons, more women are in these categories than men. The data indicate that approximately 29 percent of working women are part-timers compared to 12 percent of working men. This is also a viable workload for teenagers, and in the 16–19-year old age group, 21 percent held part-time positions. In total, 14.4 million Americans, or 14.7 percent of the work force were part-time workers in 1984, and that figure has risen. Leading employers of part-timers, such as Control Data Corporation (CDC), Hewlett-Packard, and Citibank, have very successful part-time work programs.

Part-timers may be kept on the agency's payroll for a probationary period, after which time a good worker may be hired and transferred to the regular company payroll. Also, more highly skilled part-time workers may receive more money per hour, thus compensating for benefits for which only full-time employees are eligible. A decided advantage for some individuals is that if they are not suited to the job and perform poorly, a separation does not carry the same stigma of being fired as it would for a permanent, full-time employee. A good place to find part-time work is with small, growing organizations that need people with certain skills for a limited period per week. These jobs can be found in the help-wanted sections of the newspapers, but a temporary agency might be a better place to look for a job that meets your needs.

Job-Sharing Jobs. This is a work-style in which the job responsibilities are shared by two or more individuals. According to the American Society for Training and Development, "more than 800 major American corporations will include job sharing as a job style. Those companies will gain double the creative and productive capacity in one job." Apparently, job sharing is a viable alternative to the standard workweek, for when a survey was made of 500 large- and mid-sized Seattle companies, nearly 50 percent of the respondents were willing to hire teams for full-time openings. The individuals sharing the job determine work schedules and tasks each will perform. John Naisbitt and Patricia Aburdene, the authors of *Reinventing the Corporation* recommend certain criteria that job sharers should follow:

1. Skills of each person should complement one another.
2. Partners should both be very well organized.
3. Schedules should overlap one day a week.
4. A job should be shared with someone you know.
5. Each person must be responsible for the whole job.

Contract Workers. This is a term that applies to independent workers and is frequently known as *leasing*. It is generally used by small firms or professionals who need services performed on a regular basis by personnel not on the company's payroll. Typical services that can be offered by contractual agreements are word processing, data entry, and computer programming. Contractors are self-employed and assume the usual risks of slack periods and unexpected costs involved in completing a job. By the mid-1990s, 10 million individuals will be leased employees. Firms that feel burdened with paperwork are terminating their employees and leasing them back from contracting companies. All parties seem to be benefiting: the original employer, who is relieved of the many responsibilities of personnel management; the leased employee, who receives excellent benefits; and the contracting firms, which employ thousands of people.

To support the value of these alternative work patterns, a 1987 AMS survey found that 86 percent of respondent companies use temporary employees, 77 percent use part-timers, and 59 percent use contractors.

Flextime. A concept in scheduling daily work hours for full-time employees is flextime. Although variations exist, generally personnel must work a common core of hours each day. The remaining hours that complete a day's productivity are chosen by the worker from flexible hours established by management. Many employees prefer this scheduling, for it gives them some control over time. Morale is improved, productivity increases, and absenteeism decreases. About 16 percent of the workers are now on flextime.

In conclusion, alternative work patterns in a technological society offer many benefits to both employee and employer. However, individuals opting for such work-styles must weigh the advantages and disadvantages in terms of their own preferences and personal needs.

DISADVANTAGES

There are, of course, disadvantages to becoming a clerk. An ambitious person would use the job only as a springboard to get into the business world and would do everything possible to progress to a higher level of responsibility as soon as possible. Routine work is monotonous and lacks challenge; and many clerical jobs are just a matter of keyboarding data at a terminal, maintaining files, reading, and recording data. A person who is unwilling to assume responsibility would prefer staying in a clerical position for an extended period of time.

Routine clerical jobs are very much like factory piecework in that production standards can be set and output measured. Clerks in a company with high production standards may feel that they are under too much pressure in their jobs and that the standards are unrealistic. If supervision is poor, there may be peak loads of paperwork at the end of the month, for example, which add pressure to the job.

Another disadvantage of being a clerk is salary. Because clerks' jobs have the lowest skill requirements among clerical occupations, they also are the lowest paid. The worker who doesn't eventually achieve a rating above that of clerk will remain among the lowest-paid office workers. The final disadvantage is the gradual decrease in employment opportunities for nonskilled jobs.

PROMOTION OPPORTUNITIES FOR CLERKS

Promotion opportunities are available to the employee—male or female—who qualifies, demonstrates responsibility, possesses the ability to handle challenges, performs diversified tasks, and sees the interrelatedness and importance of each task in relation to the whole. Today, capable women are advancing more rapidly than their male counterparts because of the anti-discrimination movements and the Equal Employment Opportunity Act of 1972. However, there still are disproportionate numbers of men in jobs at higher levels, while many women are still working at levels below their training or at higher levels under low-paying titles. An increasing number of firms are participating in job restructuring to offer promotional opportunities equally to both men and women.

There are no clear-cut steps up the promotion ladder in business. Some clerks may move into a classification of office assistant, then to secretary. Other clerks may move from their first position into a job as assistant to the supervisor and, eventually, into the shoes of the supervisor. Still another clerk may enter quite unrelated work after an apprenticeship—selling, for instance.

Automation has opened up new promotion opportunities for clerks. Many clerks can, with training, move from data-entry clerk to project director. The most able may be made programmers.

In well managed offices, all employees are rated periodically by their supervisors on such qualities as:

- The ability to learn new methods and techniques;
- Productiveness—the amount of work produced and how promptly it was completed;
- The neatness and accuracy with which work is performed;
- Industriousness—how consistently individuals apply their energies to their daily jobs;
- Initiative—the ability to carry out independently the appointed job and to offer suggestions for improvement;
- Cooperativeness and helpfulness—the ability to act as a team member;
- The knowledge the employee possesses of the job and related duties.

These ratings are discussed with the workers, and opportunities for improvement and for additional training may be given. A clerk who receives superior merit ratings will quickly be cited for advancement.

Most companies have a policy of promotion from within, and one of the functions of the supervisor is preparing workers for the next step upward. Many large companies offer training opportunities within the company. The first in-service courses are usually in skills; the next courses involve semisupervisory or supervisory training; and final courses are offered in the field of management itself. In cases where training inside the company seems uneconomical or impractical, arrangements sometimes are made for workers to take courses in business schools, colleges, or universities outside the company. Assistance is given in various forms—payment for books, transportation, tests, and laboratory fees; partial reimbursement for tuition at time of registration and the balance when the course is completed; full payment to the institution directly or partial payment on a sliding scale based on grade earned. In many cases, the employing company pays the full cost of these courses in order to develop employees.

A recent study on tuition-aid plans by the National Manpower Institute in Washington found that only 3 to 5 percent of white-collar workers take advantage of them, that younger workers use them more than older workers do, that women and men use them about equally, that participation increases with previous educational attainment, and that participation increases with income.

Of course, formally organized in-service courses are limited to larger companies, but smaller companies sometimes provide a wider variety of work experiences and closer association with management that compensate for the elaborate training facilities of the big corporations.

TYPES OF EQUIPMENT COMMONLY OPERATED BY CLERKS

Technological advances change the way work is performed, simultaneously increasing productivity. With these changes occurring so rapidly, it is almost impossible to keep pace. However, do not become alarmed. The basic skills learned on one machine can readily be transferred to other types of equipment. Some of the office machines most commonly operated by clerks are typewriters, dedicated word processors, microcomputers, voicewriters, copiers/duplicators/offset printers, recording/transcribing equipment, electronic calculators, facsimile equipment, optical-character readers, and Telex/TWX.

Typewriters. Conveyors of information are the documents produced and distributed in an organization. Some type of keyboarding equipment is used to produce documents such as letters, memorandums, reports, forms, contracts, minutes of meetings, and statistical tables. Basic to clerical work is the ability to type, but the degree of proficiency required depends on the job at hand.

Electric typewriters, which replaced manual machines, are still being used in many offices but are gradually being replaced by electronic typewriters. In fact, a number of manufacturers have stopped making the electric machines. The typist proficient on an electric machine can easily transfer to an electronic machine or to any terminal with a keyboard. The more modern electric typewriters have a correcting feature. Errors are corrected easily by a special lift-off tape installed in the machine very much like the ribbon.

Electronic machines are more advanced than the electric ones. Some of them have automated features such as those found on word processors: storage, memory, automatic correction, preset margins and tab stops, automatic centering, and automatic wraparound instead of the manual return at the end of each line of information. Machines vary in sophistication. Some have a one-line display, while others have a partial-page display. Some have disk drives for storage on floppy disks, while others have temporary storage only while the machine is on. Some can be connected with other equipment to send and receive communications.

Many electronic typewriters have dual pitch (10 or 12 characters to the inch) and a variety of type styles. There are keyboards for practically every language and for many different professions and businesses. For example, keyboards may be equipped with special symbols for use in the fields of astronomy, telegraphy, air navigation, electricity, medicine, pharmacy, physics, engineering, chemistry, biology, meteorology, and mathematics.

Dedicated Word Processors. These machines are primarily used for document production. The components of this equipment are the keyboard, screen or monitor, central processing unit, storage, and printer. In effect, they provide a self-contained work station. The number of copy lines that can be displayed on the screen vary from machine to machine. Some have full view of a page of text; others have a partial view. Skilled operators of this equipment have grown to appreciate its capabilities and ease of use. However, because of many factors including cost, service contracts, and space requirements, the microcomputer with word processing software is used in more offices.

Microcomputers. These machines are frequently called personal computers. They are replacing the dedicated word processors because of their versatility. The software packages range from those that perform the basic functions needed for producing correspondence to those that perform more sophisticated operations such as list processing and the integration of correspondence with other applications such as spreadsheets and graphics. The basic functions that most of the word processing packages perform are insertion, deletion, formatting, moving and copying, searching and replacing, and justifying.

Voicewriting Machines. The originator may use a voicewriting machine for dictation, and the clerk (sometimes called transcriber) may type from the record or cassette. Some machines may be attached to a telephone so that the executive may dictate from another location to a central recording and transcribing point.

Most voicewriting machines record on plastic disks or cassettes. These recordings are durable and may be mailed to a central transcribing pool or word processing center if the originator is away from the office. For instance, a salesperson may leave a customer and dictate a report from an automobile before the next call.

Via a telephone, an executive can dial the firm's central dictation system to record material, thus bypassing mail delivery. The clerk plays back the records or cassettes on a transcribing unit and types what is heard. Some newer models use microcassettes rather than regular cassettes.

A very recent innovation by Dictaphone that can enhance the transcriber's productivity is the two-line visual display on the machine, which indicates the beginning and ending of each letter, length of each letter, and special instructions.

Commonly used voicewriting machines are manufactured

under the names Dictaphone, IBM, Stenocord, Edison Voicewriter, and Lanier.

The magnetic tape cassette is very popular today. The unit is compact, and the recording media can be filed, mailed, transcribed, erased, and reused many times.

Reprographic Machines. Reprographics is the process of reproducing and duplicating letters, memorandums, reports, images, and other documents. As a clerical worker, you will probably make frequent use of a photocopier, which is generally used for shorter runs. The special features you may need to be familiar with are duplexing, or copying on both sides; reducing and enlarging copy; feeding the original pack automatically; collating; and stapling. Different processes are used for duplicating materials. The method selected depends on several criteria: quantity, quality, image, internal or external distribution, cost, and urgency in terms of time.

A copier makes copies directly from the original. The fluid and stencil processes that use prepared masters and stencils are no longer found in business environments but are still around in schools, community houses of worship, and community organizations. The offset process is used extensively for large, high-quality runs. Care should be taken in preparing the master, which is the job of the clerical worker, because the final product is an image of the original. Offset presses are placed in centralized areas, and trained personnel is necessary to operate the equipment.

The offset process is based on the fact that grease and water do not mix. The outlines on the master copy hold the printing ink, which is greasy, and the remainder of the surface attracts water and repels the ink. The ink is transferred or offset from the outline to a rubber blanket; this is what transfers the copy onto the paper. The plate may be a thick metal sheet or a paper mat, and copy may be photographed onto the plate.

Offset equipment has made inroads into many business reproduction departments because of its original-like copies, its multicolor capabilities, and its fast operating speed.

Photocopying duplicators are so nearly automatic that they

The Clerk 81

hardly require the services of skilled operators. A picture of a letter or other document may be reproduced in less than a minute. Most of the major equipment companies are producing photocopy equipment. The most common photocopy duplicator is the Xerox, although other companies are strong competitors.

The most recent technological advances in reprographics are fiber optics and laser beams. Fiber optics are thin plastic or glass rods that transmit light. Laser printers (classified as electrostatic printers) use a beam of red light to reflect characters and graphic images. The process is similar to copier technology.

Data Processing Machines. Data processing is the way in which figures are collected, manipulated (classified, sorted, integrated, recorded), and distributed. Presently, this is done through the computer. Electronic data processing systems usually consist of a combination of units including input, storage, processing, and output devices. They receive scientific or business data at electronic speeds with self-checking accuracy. Input devices record data that are transmitted into the computer. The data are stored on magnetic cassettes, tapes, or disks. The processing unit controls and governs the complete system and performs the actual arithmetic and logical operations.

The computer cannot reason or think for itself and is unable to perform even the simplest operation without definite instructions. An individual must be specially trained to operate the machine. The person who sets up the machine for analyzing data is called a programmer.

Calculating Machines. The electronic calculator is used for both personal and business purposes. It is used to add, subtract, divide, and multiply. On some machines, many calculations are simplified with an automatic constant. Operating it is a simple task, and clerical workers should be able to use it by touch.

The adding-listing machine is in demand by those individuals who want a permanent record of their calculations. The figures can be checked for errors on a paper tape on which the figures are printed.

Calculating machines record totals in the dials, from which they may be copied. They are used for addition, subtraction, multiplication, and division—all of which are practically automatic. The operator merely sets the figures on the machine and presses the proper key; the answer appears in the proper dials. Emphasis in the offices today is on the desk-size ten-key electronic calculator. Some calculators have the capacity to perform operations in multiplication and division in milliseconds, as well as square roots and statistical operations. Pocket-size calculating machines have become very popular, too.

The more sophisticated calculators have a computer-like ability to store instructions, a TV-like screen or illuminated dials to display results, and automatic decimal control.

Burroughs, Monroe, Olympia, Canon, NCR, Hewlett-Packard, and Texas Instruments manufacture many of the calculators now in use.

Facsimile Machines. These machines, also known as FAX machines, communicate information rapidly and exactly from one source to another. Although they have been around for many years, only in the past few years have they become popular as new units have become smaller and faster to operate. They also have more features than their predecessors. Text, data, graphics and photographs can be transmitted over telephone lines to a distant location in a matter of seconds. The equipment is easy to operate and takes a minimum amount of training. The facsimile equipment is used when only one copy is needed, and when time is an important factor. As reported in the article "Facsimile Offers More and Experts Tell Us Why," Hiroshi Shimoda of Canon U.S.A., Incorporated claims that by 1993 "the facsimile market should be nearly as large as the personal computer market today—five to seven million units."

To send messages from one point to another, machines have to be compatible or a computer-based system has to be installed. The FAX board, a recently developed part which connects to microcomputers, will expand communication capabilities. The public demand for FAX service is apparent when one visits a local copying center to place an order to transmit facsimiles to a particular destination.

Optical Character Recognition. This equipment, known as OCR, serves as an input device for computers and word processors. It scans typed text and handwritten characters and transfers them onto a diskette for editing on a word processor. It is being used by the postal service to scan envelopes and to sort mail by zip codes. Using OCR equipment has several advantages: no rekeying of a document is necessary and the rate of speed at which an OCR can read a typed page is much faster than the rate of keyboarding.

Not all clerks operate all of these machines. However, it is likely that a clerk will use some of them. Their operation may be learned in school, at training centers organized by the equipment manufacturers, or on the job. Proficient office machine operation is becoming increasingly important as the office becomes more and more automated.

Many companies now use computer systems for storing and retrieving important documents. (Wang Laboratories, Inc. photo)

CHAPTER 3

RECORDS MANAGEMENT: FILE CLERK TO RECORDS MANAGER

Six hundred million computer printouts, 234 million photocopies, and 76 million letters are produced each day, more than twice the amount created ten years ago, according to Art Jones in "Records Management Now & in the Future." What are the contributing factors to this paper blizzard? People are more comfortable with printed copy, something that they can hold, touch, write comments on, and show. As our economy becomes service-oriented, more information will be created, which in turn leads to growth in paper documents. More forms have to be filed and maintained for the government. As industry continues to expand into the international market, business needs to document its activities.

It is obvious, then, that these tremendous amounts of paper create a need for a well-organized, systematic approach to the management of these records. According to the *Newsletter* of the Office Systems Research Association, presently, approximately 1 percent of the information in the United States is stored using electronic and magnetic media; 4 percent is stored using microforms and optical storage techniques; and 95 percent is stored on paper. By 1996, micrographics will account for 6 percent and optical media 8 percent. Electronic methods of storage will remain at 1 percent.

The future looks bright for individuals interested in a career in records management. A hierarchy of jobs exists at levels ranging from file clerk to records clerk to records manager. Other titles include forms analyst, records supervisor, micrographics technician, records coordinator, and records analyst. What knowledge and expertise should a person have who is interested in a career in records management? An understanding and knowledge of the following systems and procedures would be beneficial:

- Filing systems: alphabetic, numeric, subject, geographic
- Computer and word processing storage
- Computer systems and capabilities
- Storage facilities and media: shelf filing, vertical carousel machines, space utilization, micrographics, microfilm feasibility studies, microform systems, computer output and input
- Information management technologies such as communicating computers
- Archive management: types, functions, evaluation
- Records retention and destruction
- Records protection

A TOTAL SYSTEMS APPROACH

Records management is a total systems approach concerned with the creation, maintenance and use, retention, transfer, and destruction of records. It is a significant area in the office and will undoubtedly continue to develop in the 1990s as it did during the past decade. The information explosion and the vast amounts of paperwork created in this electronic age have led to the creation of records centers as a vital part of a company's management program. As the volume of records grew from the mountains of information poured forth from the computer, and from the expansion of large-scale industry and government offices, clerical forces also grew to handle this paperwork, simultaneously adding new dimensions to the filing process.

Records are all documentary materials that are created or received in connection with some activity or transaction. Certain legal documents must be preserved for a stipulated period of time, while others are kept as evidence of decisions, functions, procedures, or policies used in a given situation. The many records that are commonly filed in business include correspondence, legal documents, reports, inventory lists, bank statements, price lists, maps, stockholders' records, pension records, contracts, insurance, charts, catalogs, newspaper clippings, personnel records, committee reports, and minutes. Records and information storage can be on paper, cards, punched cards, computer tapes, microfilm, microfiche, or magnetic disks.

The terms *filing* and *records management* frequently are confused. Filing is the process of arranging and storing materials according to some definite plan for immediate access and for permanence; most filing jobs are clerical in nature. Records management pertains to the life cycle of a record. This cycle includes the creation, design, processing, and disposition of records in conjunction with the selection of files and equipment and the orientation and training of employees. Records management jobs are classified as managerial.

Systems vary based on companies' needs. Some filing systems are completely automated and may be installed to rotate files horizontally on tracks or may be stacked in hidden spaces vertically in elevator-type filing consoles. Frequently, in systems such as these, operators may not have to leave their work stations.

As a substitute for paper records, microfilm has gained widespread acceptance as a recordkeeping medium. Microfilm is prepared in several formats such as roll, microfiche, aperture card, and jacket. The advantages of microfilm are that it is inexpensive both to purchase and duplicate, and it is readily stored in compact office files from which it is also easily retrieved.

Most office workers, including supervisors, managers, and executives, do some filing. In small firms, the work is usually performed by the secretaries and stenographers; in large firms, clerks usually do the bulk of the filing. These large firms have centralized record areas.

Since businesses of every size use records, filing jobs can be found almost anywhere in the United States. Some of the specialized job titles for entry-level work are: coding clerk, records clerk, unit clerk, sorting clerk, correspondence file clerk, and file clerk. The U.S. Bureau of Labor Statistics describes the levels of file clerks as follows:

Clerk, File I. Performs routine filing of material that has already been classified or which is easily classified in a simple serial classification system (e.g., alphabetical, chronological, or numerical). As requested, locates readily available material in files and forwards material; may fill out withdrawal charge. May perform simple clerical and manual tasks required to maintain and service files

Clerk, File II. Sorts, codes, and files unclassified material by simple (subject matter) headings or partly classified material by finer subheadings. Prepares simple related index and cross-reference aids. As requested, locates clearly identified material in files and forwards material. May perform related clerical tasks required to maintain and service files.

Clerk, File III. Classifies and indexes file material such as correspondence, reports, technical documents, etc., in an established filing system containing a number of varied subject matter files. May also file this material. May keep records of various types in conjunction with the files. May lead a small group of lower level file clerks.

Some of the responsibilities of the specialized clerks are:

Correspondence File Clerk. Maintains a file of general correspondence; sorts and files; answers inquiries about correspondence; maintains a follow-up file; labels folders; retrieves correspondence; and maintains an activity-count record.

Sorting Clerk. Handles notices of change; distributes changes to unit clerks; alphabetizes information on new accounts; sorts outgoing interoffice communications; types envelopes; and routes caption changes and changes of address to the central file records.

Unit Clerk. Maintains an alphabetical unit of customer cards; answers inquiries about customers; processes reports and data about accounts; handles signature cards for the file; checks against file for titles of officers of customer accounts; and removes cards from unit file according to a retention schedule.

Coding Clerk. Codes information obtained from reports for processing by machines.

Records Clerk. Receives company records and examines contents to determine filing captions; maintains a card file of records by data for destruction; locates information in central files upon request; and assists supervisor in organization of records and filing procedures.

Records Managers. Supervises and trains personnel in maintenance of central files; supervises work of employees and evaluates performance; improves personnel relations in the records management department; keeps monthly records of activity; performs miscellaneous duties.

Promotional opportunities are available to the alert, well-trained clerk who knows how to file and control records. The employee who uses initiative and demonstrates leadership qualities may rise from the entry-level job of file clerk to the position of file supervisor, file consultant, or the highly responsible position of a records manager. Most employers follow a promotion-from-within policy.

EMPLOYMENT AND SALARIES

In 1986 approximately 242,000 file clerks were employed. Projected estimates for 2000 indicate there will be a demand for 274,000 such employees, a 13 percent increase in employment. Although the increased demand for recordkeeping will result in job openings, the growth rate is not expected to be as rapid as in past years because of the increasing use of electronic computers for filing and retrieving information.

File clerks are the foundation of the records system of a business. However, in spite of their vital function, they are among the lowest-paid office employees. Of the eight clerical jobs surveyed as of March, 1986, by the U.S. Bureau of Labor Statistics, the beginning file clerks I were at the bottom salary level, earning an average of less than $861 per month. Experienced file clerks III received salaries above accounting clerks II but below key entry operators II and typist II. The average annual salary for the year ending March, 1986, was $10,335 for file clerk I; $12,156 for file clerk II; and $15, 625 for file clerk III. The projected weekly increase in clerical salaries for 1987 throughout the nation was 5.2 percent. See Chart 7 for a comparison of salaries for various clerical positions.

CHART 7
Average Salaries for Clerical Occupations
March 1986

Job Title	1980 Annual Salary	1986 Annual Salary
Clerks, Accounting I	8,806	12,517
Clerks, Accounting II	10,877	14,687
Clerks, Accounting III	12,328	17,954
Clerks, Accounting IV	15,358	21,872
File Clerks I	7,889	10,335
File Clerks II	8,829	12,156
File Clerks III	11,026	15,625
Key Entry Operators I	9,981	13,146
Key Entry Operators II	11,723	16,901
Messengers	8,561	12,276
Typists I	9,161	12,584
Typists II	11,010	16,854
Personnel Clerks I	9,591	14,193
Personnel Clerks II	11,529	16,903
Personnel Clerks III	12,896	19,696
Personnel Clerks IV	15,726	23,702
General Clerks I*	N/A	10,478
General Clerks II	N/A	12,730
General Clerks III	N/A	15,500
General Clerks IV	N/A	19,322
Stenographers I	11,899	18,374
Stenographers II	13,876	21,739

Based on Bureau of Labor Statistics, National Survey of Professional, Administrative, Technical and Clerical Pay (Bulletin 2271, October, 1986.)
*A four-level general clerk job was introduced in 1986.

EDUCATIONAL REQUIREMENTS AND PERSONAL APTITUDES

Most employers prefer to hire high school graduates for beginning file clerk jobs. They prefer applicants who can type, have a knowledge of office practices, have an aptitude for numbers, have the ability to do detailed work accurately, and are able to read quickly and with understanding. In addition, employees should understand the importance to management of accurate files, the necessity to follow organized procedures, and the importance of teamwork. Good clerks have manual dexterity, good eyesight, and good memories. Since file clerks have access to the confidential records of the company, they should possess the personal qualifications expected of other office workers—loyalty to the firm and ability to keep confidences.

THE FUTURE

Records management is vital because information has become an important resource in decision making. Users of this information will place greater demands for instant retrieval of data, and this can best be accomplished through a managed system of records. Certain trends are evident that support this theory: universal usage of computers; computer output microfilm recorders; appearance of video disks, lasers, fiber optics; computer-assisted retrieval devices; and use of multimode media. Although records management is not glamorous, many individuals will be vying for top positions. The best route to take is to learn about the functions, procedures, equipment, and media used. Equally as important is to develop good leadership skills, to understand principles of supervision, to maintain good human relations, to be well organized, to learn the terminology, and to understand the broad field of information and records management.

Some secretaries are expected to perform computer-oriented tasks dealing with financial applications, spreadsheet applications, database management, and graphics. (IBM photo)

CHAPTER 4

INFORMATION/WORD PROCESSING: THE SECRETARY

A 1988 help-wanted ad survey reveals 25.6 percent more ads for secretaries than in 1987, according to Kay Fusselman's article in *The Secretary*. Business, professional offices, and government need qualified, competent individuals with good communications, administrative, organizational, typing, and word processing skills.

In this revised edition, the position of stenographer no longer appears in the title of this chapter because of the sharp decline in demand. Nevertheless, since a considerable number of job opportunities are still available, according to the U.S. Bureau of Labor Statistics, it deserves attention for those interested in this kind of employment. However, a review of the help-wanted ads in the newspapers reveals a dearth of these positions as separate listings. Perhaps stenographic jobs are subsumed under the secretarial category. When considering a stenographic position, examine it realistically in view of market trends.

Chapter 1 indicated that the demand for stenographers is declining, and projections reflect a 28 percent decrease in employment between 1986 and 2000. The widespread use of dictation machines accounts for this reduction in stenographers. However, the demand will be great for shorthand reporters because of the rising number of criminal court cases and lawsuits in the state and federal courts.

94   *Opportunities in Office Occupations*

Secretarial responsibilities go far beyond typing, filing, and transcribing and extend into personnel administration, supervision, and management. The office as it is now and as it will evolve will require new secretarial skills, knowledge, and attitudes to meet the challenges created by technology. The most common job title in the word processing category is *secretary,* the subject of this chapter.

In the past, the skill that distinguished stenographers and secretaries from clerks was their knowledge of shorthand. That skill is still required of all individuals seeking jobs as stenographers but not necessarily of secretaries. A glance at the help-wanted section of *The New York Times* on two typical Sundays confirms this statement. Of the 218 secretarial positions advertised one Sunday, on just one page, 17 asked for shorthand skills and two ads stated "with or without steno." Of the 17 ads with shorthand, two stated "steno or fast longhand." On the second Sunday, of the 234 ads for secretaries, 25 specified shorthand, and two ads, with or without shorthand. Generally, ads specified good typing and word processing skills. Some even requested experience on specific hardware and software, for example: IBM PC, Word Perfect, Displaywrite 4. Another indication of the decrease in shorthand use is reflected in a 1987 study of secretaries in which only 24 percent of the respondents stated that they use shorthand every day. For further discussion of shorthand, see Chapter 5.

More realistically, secretaries can be distinguished from clerks by the professional tasks secretaries now perform. Tasks previously within the sole domain of managers are now being delegated to secretaries, especially the computer-oriented tasks dealing with financial applications, spreadsheet applications, database management, and graphics. As reported in "Computers Ease the Load—At Times," Larry Hirschhorn, a research fellow at the Wharton School, claims that "office technology links previously unconnected tasks such as typing and editing of research and graphics production and thus is transforming many secretarial jobs into 'paraprofessional' careers. Technology integrates what were traditionally divided skills."

According to the *National Survey of Professional, Administra-*

tive, Technical, and Clerical Pay, March 1986 (Bulletin 2271, U.S. Department of Labor, Bureau of Labor Statistics), the specific tasks performed by stenographers and secretaries are as follows:

> *Stenographer.* Primary duty is to take dictation using shorthand, and to transcribe the dictation. May also type from written copy. May operate from a stenographic pool. May occasionally transcribe from voice recordings.

Note: This job is differentiated from that of a secretary in that a secretary normally works as the principal secretarial support performing more responsible and discretionary tasks.

A level I stenographer takes and transcribes dictation, receiving specific assignments along with detailed instructions on such requirements as forms and presentation and performs routine clerical tasks under close supervision.

A level II stenographer performs stenographic duties requiring significantly greater independence and responsibility than stenographer I; maintains follow-up files; assembles material for reports, memoranda, and letters; composes simple letters from general instructions; reads and routes incoming mail; and answers routine questions.

> *Secretary.* Provides principal secretarial support in an office, usually to one individual, and in some cases to the subordinate staff of that individual. Maintains a close and highly responsible relationship to the day-to-day activities of the supervisor and staff. Works fairly independently, receiving a minimum of detailed supervision and guidance. Performs varied clerical and secretarial duties requiring a knowledge of office routine and understanding of the organization, programs, and procedures related to the work of the office.

The level of the secretary's responsibility (LR) dictates the nature of the work relationship between the secretary and the supervisor and the extent to which the secretary is expected to exercise initiative and judgment. Another factor that impacts classification is the level of the secretary's supervisor within the overall organizational structure.

LR–1. Works under general instructions and guidance; carries out *recurring* office procedures independently. Performs duties comparable to the following: maintains supervisor's calendar; handles the telephone; makes appointments; reviews correspondence for typographical accuracy and proper format; maintains recurring internal reports having to do with time and leave records, training plans, and office equipment listings; requisitions supplies; takes and transcribes dictation; and maintains office files.

LR–2. Works independently and in addition to LR–1 responsibilities, performs tasks requiring greater judgment, initiative, and knowledge of office functions. Some of the duties include screening calls; writing and signing routine, nontechnical correspondence; handles meeting arrangements; and coordinates personnel and administrative forms.

LR–3. In addition to LR–1 and LR–2 responsibilities, handles nonroutine situations; interprets and adapts guidelines. Duties include: composing correspondence on own initiative for supervisor's approval; anticipates and prepares materials needed for correspondence and meetings; under general direction, excerpts material from documents in preparation of special or one-time reports; refers to supervisor for consideration of important publication items.

LR–4. At this level, the secretary handles a wide variety of situations and conflicts involving the clerical or administrative functions of the office, particularly when the executive is not available. Additional duties of the position include composing and signing correspondence, assigning staff members to attend meetings, establishing priorities, and summarizing contents of incoming mail.

The long-standing definition of *secretary* adopted by Professional Secretaries International refers more to the personal qualities required for success than to the specific tasks enumerated above. A secretary is:

> An assistant to an executive who possesses mastery of office skills and ability to assume responsibility without direct supervision, displays initiative, exercises judgment, and makes decisions within the scope of assigned authority.

Within this concept, a secretary is a highly qualified person who possesses not only "mastery of office skills" but also personality traits of the highest order. The secretary discharges the responsibilities for which he or she has authority, and is a creative, responsible individual capable of making many decisions.

In 1978, a survey of firms, ranging from small to large in both the private and public sectors, was conducted by Professional Secretaries International (then known as National Secretaries Association, NSA) to develop a prototype secretarial job description, which appears below.

> A secretary relieves executive of various administrative details; coordinates and maintains effective office procedures and efficient work flows; implements policies and procedures set by employer; establishes and maintains harmonious working relationships with superiors, coworkers, subordinates, customers or clients, and suppliers.
>
> Schedules appointments and maintains calendar. Receives and assists visitors and telephone callers and refers them to executive or other appropriate person as circumstances warrant. Arranges business itineraries and coordinates executive's travel requirements.
>
> Takes action authorized during executive's absence and uses initiative and judgment to see that matters requiring attention are referred to delegated authority or handled in a manner so as to minimize effect of employer's absence.
>
> Takes manual shorthand and transcribes from it or transcribes from machine dictation. Types material from longhand or rough copy.
>
> Sorts, reads, and annotates incoming mail and documents and attaches appropriate file to facilitate necessary action; determines routing, signatures required, and maintains follow-up. Composes correspondence and reports for own or executive's signature. Prepares communication outlined by executive in oral or written directions.
>
> Researches and abstracts information and supporting data in preparation for meetings, work projects, and reports. Correlates and edits materials submitted by others. Organizes material which may be presented to executive in draft format.
>
> Maintains filing and records management systems and other office flow procedures.
>
> Makes arrangements for and coordinates conferences and meetings. May serve as recorder of minutes with responsibility for transcription and distribution to participants.

May supervise or hire other employees; select and/or make recommendations for purchase of supplies and equipment; maintain budget and expense account records, financial records, and confidential files.

Maintains up-to-date procedures manual for the specific duties handled on the job.

Performs other duties as assigned or as judgment or necessity dictates.

This prototype description is still valid today, with certain modifications and additions. Findings from the 1987 PSI member profile survey, which appeared in Kay Fusselman's "Secretaries: A Profile," revealed that shorthand usage has declined and computer usage by secretaries has increased. A summary of the results of this survey that have relevance to the prototype description follows.

- Only 24 percent of the secretaries use shorthand each day, although 90 percent of the respondents can write shorthand.
- Since 1982, the number of secretaries using computer-based equipment has tripled. Approximately 60 percent are using electronic typewriters; 48 percent, word processors; 42 percent, personal computers; and 26 percent, terminals/workstations.
- Forty-eight percent work for large organizations, more than 500 employees, compared to 30 percent in 1979.
- Ninety-five percent of the respondents have finished some type of postsecondary education, compared to 83 percent in 1982. Of this number, approximately 40 percent completed a secretarial program at a two-year college; 43 percent have some college credit; and 10 percent have a bachelor's degree.
- Employers prefer secretaries who are specialists in certain areas. Results indicated 55 percent were in administration.

EMPLOYMENT OUTLOOK FOR SECRETARIES

One of the most important considerations in making a career choice is the availability of jobs when the education and training are completed and you are ready to enter the labor market. To see the great shortage of *secretaries,* a person only has to look at the openings in the help-wanted columns of the daily newspaper. For example, even when the national rate of unemployment was 5.6 percent in May 1988, on a "light" day in *The New York Times,* more than 115 openings were advertised for secretaries versus 5 advertisements for typists and 72 for bookkeepers.

A periodic check of the newspapers will indicate local needs, but even more reliable is the work of the U.S. Department of Labor, which forecasts where jobs will be found in the next 10–14 years. It reports that 700,000 new secretarial positions will become available within the next decade. The spring 1988 issue of the *Occupational Outlook Quarterly* unveils employment estimates for approximately 500 occupations. The total employment rate for secretaries, which was 3,234,000 in 1986, will rise to 4,648,000 by the year 2000, or an increase of 13 percent. For stenographers, employment figures will decline from 178,000 to 128,000, a decrease of 28 percent. The demand for secretarial workers is still 9 percent higher than for bookkeepers/accounting clerks. See Chart 8 for comparisons in growth and decline of these clerical positions.

NEW INNOVATIONS IN RECRUITMENT

It is important to note that while the demand for secretaries is great, there exists a shortage of qualified candidates for these positions. Several large firms have resorted to holding an open house to recruit new employees. Many are also advertising Keogh plans, excellent health and dental benefits, and good vacations. Another innovative approach is "mentoring," whereby a senior member of a firm provides counseling and career guidance to a new employee. Companies find that employee turnover is reduced and that the new employee feels more closely identified with the organization. This strategy also creates good morale, helps instill confidence, and helps a person cope with difficult situations.

CHART 8
Percentage Growth and Decline of New Workers 1986–2000

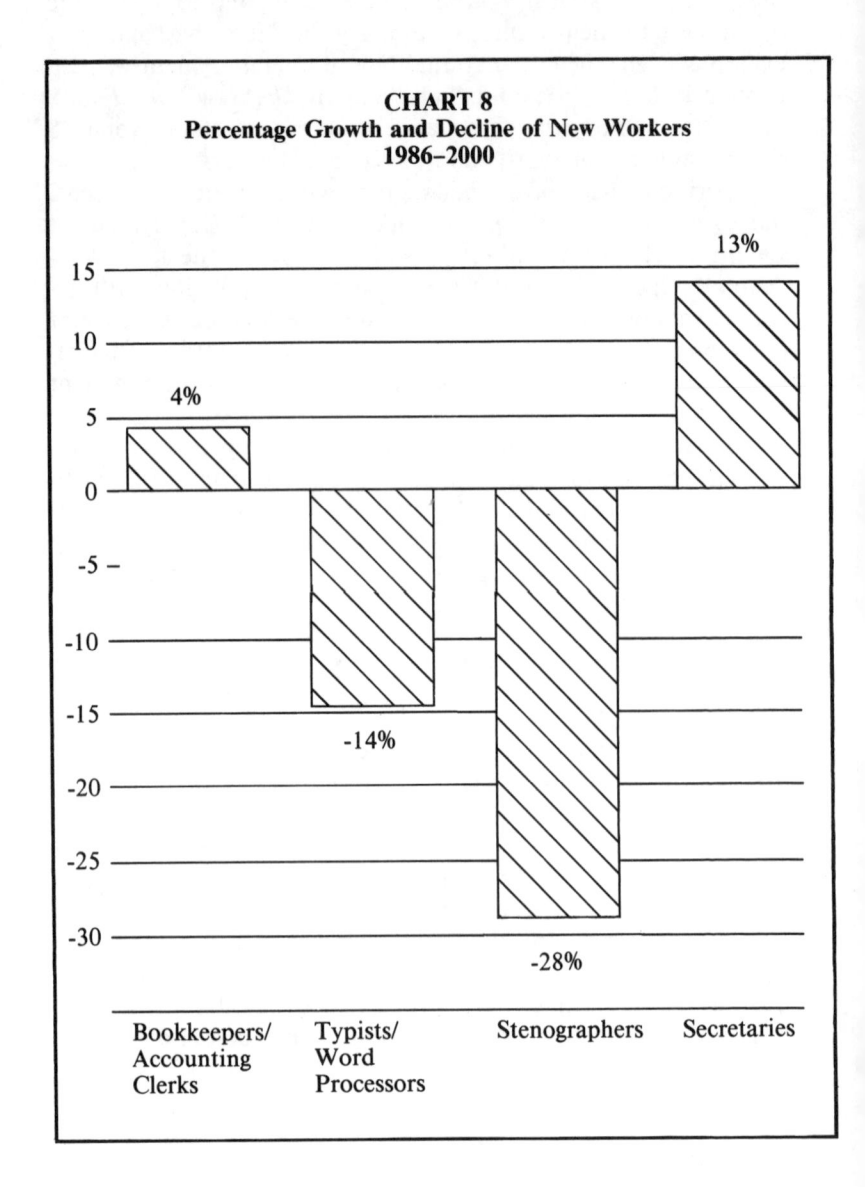

Occupation	Percentage
Bookkeepers/Accounting Clerks	4%
Typists/Word Processors	-14%
Stenographers	-28%
Secretaries	13%

SALARIES

The area wage surveys researched by the U.S. Department of Labor, Bureau of Labor Statistics, provide information about salaries. Of course, wages in large cities are usually higher than those in small towns. Also, salaries paid in the west are generally the highest in the nation. However, according to the findings of a Temp Force, Incorporated, survey of 140,000 employees nationwide, reported in "Average Entry-Level Clerical Salaries Rise," the Northeast recorded the largest projected increase for 1988, 5.8 percent, compared to the Midwest at 5.3 percent, the Southeast at 4.9 percent, and the West at 4.4 percent. A review of the figures will give you some idea of how the salaries of secretaries and stenographers compare with those of other office workers.

Following are the average weekly salaries for office workers in the Richmond, Virginia metropolitan area as of June 1987; the Milwaukee, Wisconsin metropolitan area as of May 1987; and the San Francisco, California metropolitan area as of March 1987. (See Chart 9.)

It is significant that with the exception of systems analysts and programmers—who are usually classified as professionals—secretaries and stenographers lead the salaries of the office force, $365–479 for secretaries and $371–396 for stenographers.

A final comment about salaries reflects the upward trend. A 1987 survey of members of Professional Secretaries International, who had been employed as secretaries for at least five years, indicated that an estimated average annual salary is $20,650 compared to an average of $17,440 in 1982, representing a 4 percent annual increase. Interestingly, the average annual salary of members of Professional Secretaries International is higher than the average for all secretaries, according to the U.S. Bureau of Labor Statistics.

CHART 9
Average Weekly Salaries of Office Workers
1987

Title	Richmond, Virginia Metropolitan Area June 1987	Milwaukee Metropolitan Area May 1987	San Francisco Metropolitan Area March 1987
Systems Analyst	$685.50	$693.00	$752.00
Programmer	522.00	506.50	682.00
Secretary IV	421.00	426.00	479.00
Stenographer	371.00	396.50	—
Secretary	365.00	371.00	456.50
Computer Operator	352.50	376.50	431.00
Order Clerk	337.50	320.00	359.50
Word Processor	308.50	303.50	402.00
Payroll Clerk	304.00	333.00	422.50
Accounting Clerk	291.50	289.50	412.00
Receptionist	274.50	255.50	311.50
Typist	267.50	298.00	399.00
Key Entry Operator	260.00	265.00	359.00
Switchboard Operator	252.00	268.50	316.00
File Clerk	205.50	214.00	264.50

A DECADE OF CHANGE: WHAT SECRETARIES SAY!

Secretarial work is a rewarding, exciting career as attested to by several secretaries who have been actively employed since the beginning of this decade.

Nancy DeMars, 1980–81 international president of Professional Secretaries International, says:

> "The career of the *professional secretary* has become one of the most exciting and fulfilling in the business world today. Due to the acute secretarial shortage of this decade and the expansion of secretarial responsibilities within the business structure, the career secretary now finds herself/himself an integral part of a company's operations.
>
> "If one wishes to be a *professional secretary* (and use the profession as a steppingstone to another career), what better way to learn the business than via the secretarial profession. However, if one

wishes to pursue the professional secretarial position as a career in itself, the recognition/rewards are now increasing rapidly.

"In order to meet the opportunities available today, the *professional secretary* must become thoroughly trained and educated (and this means *beyond* the high school level). Shorthand is essential (for the top echelon offices); and you must have proficient skills, a proper command of written and spoken English, and a fundamental knowledge of general office procedures. Also, you must be well-groomed at all times; and you must be able to know how to get along with people at all levels.

"On-the-job hints: Anticipate what lies ahead (anticipate your executive and the situations before you). Fully understand the scope of your authority (write your own job description if there is none established), and continually let your superiors know you are willing to assume additional responsibilities. Use your initiative and judgment; and be unflappable (expect the unexpected). Be an innovator and always maintain an objective and progressive attitude.

"Think professional, act professional, and be professional! One way to prove your professionalism beyond question is by the pursuit of the Certified Professional Secretary rating. An annual two-day, six-part examination tests all areas of the secretarial position. If you are serious about achieving status as a *professional secretary,* set your sights on this goal now."

In "Secretaries Come of Age in the Eighties," Angela Angerosa puts it this way: "Twenty years ago, a secretary typed, filed, answered phones, and took dictation. Not anymore. Today's secretaries have a much wider repertoire of skills, are more a part of the management team, and ambitious, to boot."

Angerosa reports that Shelly Ballet, director of marketing for the Katharine Gibbs School, New York City, views secretaries as "partners, working side by side with their bosses and taking responsibility for more decision-making tasks." Ballet believes opportunities for growth are enormous.

Angerosa also quotes Terrie Nagle, CPS, administrative assistant at Sundstrand-Sauer Company, Ames, Iowa, who says her position offers her a "more relaxed working environment and a greater sense of freedom."

In "Today's Secretary: Moving Up," Eleanor P. Vreeland, president of Katharine Gibbs School and vice-president of MacMillan, Inc., says that "today's professionals are moving up the career ladder into various positions of increased authority and responsibility." Many fascinating and challenging career opportunities are available to secretaries. However, hard work, perseverance, commitment, and enthusiasm toward one's job are the key attributes for achievement and recognition. Technological advances have made it easier for secretaries to be recognized. Now, more time can be spent on composing correspondence instead of typing it. Statistical reports no longer have to be typed from a draft; secretaries may use a spreadsheet program to prepare the information.

Adella C. LaRue, international president of Professional Secretaries International, in her address at the 1987 convention on the "State of the Profession," phrased her beliefs succinctly when she said, "The secretarial profession in 1987 is alive and well and more dynamic, more exciting than ever."

Frances Barr gives some sound advice to secretaries. "Set some sights for yourselves. Never let your vision of success fade, because when your vision fades, so does opportunity."

"Change is the only constant," says Carol Kinsey Gorman, in "Change and the Secretary of the Future." "[y]ou have already been affected by the rapid advancements in technology, robotics, electronic workstations, artificial intelligence, and software.... Crucial to the success of a secretary is the ability to adapt to change and to thrive on it."

THE CHANGING ROLE OF THE SECRETARY

As technology was introduced into the office, simultaneously the nature of the work being performed and the role of the secretary changed. New job titles were established, new position requirements evolved, work flow was reorganized, and office procedures became automated.

A survey by Katharine Gibbs School of its graduates, secretaries, and businesses, cited in LaRue's "State of the Profession" address, found that 93 percent of the respondents concur that the role of the secretary has undergone changes: 75 percent see word processing as having the greatest impact on the secretary's role; computer literacy is vital; 60 percent visualize the field of computers as the leading growth industry in which secretaries can advance; secretaries are assuming more administrative responsibilities; good writing and communication skills are necessary; open-mindedness, adaptability, organizational skills, and the ability to analyze and solve problems are prerequisites of the job.

In "Knowledge Management: Opportunity for the Secretary of the Future," Paul Strassman speaks of the intangibles of the secretarial role. Knowledge management, an intangible, has always been handled by secretaries. The difference now is that electronic tools are available to lighten the task. He states that knowing how individual tasks such as taking messages, scheduling, filing, copying, and typing can all be connected for a particular use is what creates value, not individual functions. Most important, however, is to understand the implications of these activities on the success of the organization. Secretaries need to use computers to manage these connections by developing database management and information-retrieval systems. A secretary's primary value to an organization is through "electronics-aided management of recorded knowledge."

PROMOTION OPPORTUNITIES FOR SECRETARIES

For many years, working in a secretarial job was a steppingstone to higher-level office positions and even alternate careers. For others, secretarial work fulfilled the dreams of a satisfying, lifetime occupation. A 1986 study of highly successful business women by Boyden International, an executive recruiting firm, attests to the former statement. The study found that almost 40 percent of the women began their careers in secretarial positions and 16 percent as management trainees.

The 1970s were the beginning of phenomenal changes in the employment picture. Affirmative Action legislation increased opportunities for women. Companies, particularly those involved in federal government contracts, were forced not to discriminate against women and minority groups in terms of employment and promotions. Undoubtedly, many an executive faced with the possibility of court action for violations began hiring and promoting qualified female workers. During the years when there was tremendous growth in office employment, many women were moved up into managerial positions. What were some of the assets these women possessed so that they would be recognized? In addition to doing a good job, an employee has to be visible, be willing to take on a challenge, have good interpersonal and good communication skills, be able to delegate responsibility, and be creative.

A sampling of former secretaries who were promoted in recent years attests to the importance of these qualities: Jodi Owens was made senior vice-president of corporate finance for Shearson-Lehman Brothers; Eleanor P. Vreeland, became president of the Katharine Gibbs School and vice-president of MacMillan, Incorporated; Donna Mather was promoted to office manger for the Tech Center Branch of Rothgerber, Appel, Powers & Johnson in Denver; Lee Ann Nay became administrator-external communications for GTE North Incorporated in Westfield, Indiana; and Sharon Facchin was made personnel supervisor of Monsanto Enviro-Chem Systems, Incorporated, in St. Louis, Missouri.

In all fairness, though, it must be pointed out that new entry-level management jobs for women are opening up. Women are being hired for more and more jobs in all categories of the business world, including management. Today, a woman secretary attempting to advance her career will find new competition with other women who earn their advancement via another path.

LIMITING FACTORS IN SECRETARIAL CAREERS

In the traditional secretarial framework, the secretarial title follows the boss's title, not the worker's ability. The secretary is sometimes rated a secretary B rather than a secretary A because of the status of his or her superior, not because of his or her competence.

Another limiting factor is the different connotations of the word *secretary*. To attract applicants, a company will advertise for a secretary when the work is purely stenographic or even clerical. Then, too, *secretary* is a status symbol. Who ever heard an employer speak of "my stenographer" or "my clerk?" No, the reference is always to "my secretary." Even within a company, the executives have such a different concept of the term that one boss will assign a wide range of responsibilities, while another will make such limited use of the secretary's abilities that the job becomes frustrating.

The final limiting factor is the necessity for the secretary to become totally involved with the employer's problems. As one secretary said candidly, "If I ever quit, it will be because I'm tired of thinking other people's thoughts and want to work on my own." The secretary is working with somebody else's ideas and is the person through whom these ideas are presented and implemented.

With the advent of office systems, however, opportunities have proliferated for professional growth for secretaries. They can more easily broaden their activities, learn sophisticated software applications, and help design and implement new procedures.

With the secretarial shortage that now exists, a knowledgeable, personable, skillful secretary has unlimited opportunities for advancement. A limiting factor, however, exists for those who work for several principals, which is more commonplace today than in the past. Secretaries now have to adjust to the characteristics of each of the individuals for whom they work as well as learn to prioritize and handle delicate situations concerning workload.

EDUCATIONAL PREPARATION

Occupational education is given at all educational levels from the high school up. Programs are designed to prepare youth and adults for entry-level employment—and with further education—for career mobility.

In the past, most high schools offered a specialization in the field, and the usual curriculum included, along with some nonspecialized courses, English (three or four years), typewriting (two years), shorthand and transcription (two years), and secretarial practice (one year or one semester). The basic curriculum was varied in some schools with the inclusion of such courses as bookkeeping, business mathematics, data processing, business law, or business organizations. More recently, school boards and state departments of education have been evaluating their business and marketing sequences in response to the changing workplace and the demands of an information/technological age. Some districts have revamped curricula to provide all students in all specializations with a well-grounded education in the following broad, transferable skills that are deemed to be most important in our complex society: communications, human relations, decision making, computer literacy, basic economic concepts, applied math, personal resource management, and data manipulation.

In New York State, students who desire a regents endorsed diploma are required to complete four years of English and social studies and two years of science and math in addition to language, art, music, hygiene, and health education courses. Added to this general core of subjects is a three-unit, five-unit, or a five-to-six-unit job preparation sequence. Some of the courses for students interested in secretarial careers are: introduction to occupations, keyboarding, keyboarding applications, business communications, shorthand/transcription, electronic information processing, advanced electronic information processing, business analysis/business computer applications, and financial information processing.

Some high schools have readjusted class schedules for business preparatory courses to provide extended time frames for students to complete their assignments. A block program of two or three periods frequently replaces the usual 40- or 50-minute class. Many schools are offering advanced work through projects involving simulations in place of advanced keyboarding and shorthand. Such projects are used to bridge the gap between the real world and school. Realistic jobs are used for classroom activities, with students fulfilling tasks normally required of office personnel in varied positions. Thus, students see relationships between their own individual jobs and those of other office workers. Another advantage of simulations is that students receive training in office behavior, an aspect often overlooked in traditional classrooms.

Since the 1960s, two-year community colleges have grown into a major training ground for secretaries. Since one of the objectives of these colleges is to prepare students for semiprofessional jobs, practically all of them offer a secretarial program. However, many institutions have changed the names of their departments to reflect the trend in automated offices. Whereas some were typically called department of secretarial studies or secretarial science department, newer titles used include secretarial/office administration department, department of office technologies, and business office administration and technology. Some of the reasons for the changes were to attract males into this specialization and to announce that the instructional programs provided education and training in the latest technology. Here is one such program for an individual who wishes to be an executive secretary, which is offered at Bronx Community College in New York City:

First Semester
Fundamental Composition
History of the Modern World
Shorthand 1 (Gregg)
Typewriting 1
Business Mathematics
Fundamental Communication

Second Semester
Science Course
Intro. to Data Processing or
 Fundamental Accounting 1
Intro. to Mathematical Thought
Shorthand 2 (Gregg)
Typewriting 2
Physical Education - Activity Course

Third Semester
Any course in Art or Music
Business Communications
Shorthand 3 (Gregg)
Typewriting 3

Machine Transcription 1
Free Elective

Fourth Semester
Shorthand 4 (Gregg)
Secretarial Practice
Word Processing Administration
Cooperative Work Experience
Social Science Elective
Free Elective
Senior Orientation

Below is the secretarial science curriculum for the Community College Component of West Virginia State College in Institute, West Virginia, which was developed for all students.

First Semester
Intermediate Typewriting
Intermediate Shorthand
Business Mathematics or
　College Algebra
Introduction to Business
Effective Communication
Career Planning

Second Semester
Advanced Typewriting
Advanced Dictation
Technical Writing or
　Effective Communication
Principles of Economics or
　Social Science Elective
Introduction to Humanities
Restricted Elective from Elements of
　Supervision, Personal Finance, Writing
　for Business

Third Semester
First-Year Accounting

Word Processing Concepts
Survey of Computers and
　Programming
Business Law I or
　Introduction to Health Care
　(Medical Option)
Advanced Dictation and Transcription or
　Legal Dictation and Terminology or
　(Legal Option)
　Medical Dictation and Terminology
　(Medical Option)

Fourth Semester
First-Year Accounting
Secretarial and Office Procedures
Restrictive Elective
　Legal Secretary (Legal Option)
　Medical Transcription (Medical Option)
Business Internship or Cooperative
　Education or
　Elements of Supervision, or Personal Finance,
　or Writing for Business (Executive or Medical
　Option)
Word Processing Applications

With the explosion of office systems dealing with information processing and word processing, many colleges have either integrated these concepts with equipment training in existing courses or have designed new courses that all secretarial students are required to take to prepare themselves for changing environments. Many of the schools are equipped with dedicated word processors and microcomputers. Some schools have networked-based systems to create, edit, reproduce, and communicate all types of documents. Others have developed programs in telecommunications and desk-top publishing. Software packages used for instruction include word processing, spreadsheet applications, and database management. These are tasks performed by a growing number of employed secretaries.

In addition to public two-year colleges, private two-year colleges offer one- and two-year secretarial programs. Private business schools, many of them accredited, are a primary source for business training. In some of these schools, students may enroll at any time, not necessarily at the beginning of the term, and may progress at their own rates.

In addition to the school programs already described, secretarial courses are offered in almost all continuing education programs—at the YMCA, in evening high schools and colleges, in churches, in lodges, in company training programs and wherever self-improvement is the goal. Business organizations also are forced by shortages of secretaries to offer in-service courses. It is not uncommon for clerks to enroll in company courses in shorthand, typewriting, and word processing in the hope of being promoted to secretarial/administrative support positions. Secretaries frequently are sent to company-sponsored courses in English, proofreading, and business writing.

SPECIALIZED SECRETARIAL JOBS

Four secretarial positions require specialized abilities: legal secretary, medical secretary, technical secretary, and public stenographer.

Legal Secretary. Because the vocabulary of law is highly specialized and matters of form and procedure so complicated, many community colleges offer special courses in legal shorthand along with special content courses in legal background. However, many regular secretaries receive their specialized training in legal work on the job from legal secretaries working in the same department.

Legal secretaries prepare correspondence and legal documents such as motions, subpoenas, summonses, complaints, contracts, and wills. They have to understand legal procedures and be able to maintain accurate records. Errors can be extremely expensive.

Secretaries may review law journals and assist in legal research.

The work of the law office is exacting. The hours are long, and much of the work is performed under pressure. It is no surprise, then, that legal secretaries are among the highest paid in the field.

Medical Secretary. A supervisor of secretaries in a medical department of one of the largest hospitals in New York City stated the case this way: "A good medical secretary is worth her/his weight in gold." This person must have excellent communication skills, must type 60–65 words per minute, must transcribe heavy loads of recorded dictation, and must know medical terminology. In this particular facility, a six-week training program is given to all new recruits, who are part of a support system in which senior medical secretaries guide and counsel the new entrants.

Courses in medical shorthand as well as in medical terminology and medical office procedures are given in community colleges. A medical secretary may act as a receptionist for a doctor and may even handle billing. Some even perform such medical duties as taking temperatures and blood pressures.

Technical Secretary. The "tech sec" works for the scientist or the engineer, employers who are at home in the laboratory but not in the office. They are likely, then, to leave much of the organization of the office to the secretary and expect him or her to handle much of the routine. In addition to usual secretarial duties, the "tech sec" prepares most of the mail from composition to mailing, maintains the technical library, gathers materials for scientific papers and types and edits them, and is more of an assistant than secretary. The engineering secretary checks specifications in contracts against standards and orders the materials that meet the specifications. The work is very demanding, but the pay is high. A good knowledge of and interest in mathematics and science are useful assets for the "tech sec."

Public Stenographer. Secretaries interested in working on their own may open offices as public stenographers. The offices are usually located in a hotel near prospective employers who need special services, usually in a hurry. Public stenographers serve only those who bring work to them; and because they usually do only small jobs for a traveling population of employers, they can charge rather high rates for piecework. Public stenographers are usually also notary publics, those authorized by the state to witness signatures. For this service, they receive a small fee. Much of their work is of a legal nature, and secretaries contemplating careers as public stenographers should be experienced in legal work.

The major advantages of becoming a public stenographer are freedom from supervision and a wide variety of work assignments. One never knows what type of job will be brought in. If the public stenographer is located in a good spot, he or she may expect to made a good salary.

The disadvantages of becoming a public stenographer are the instability of employment and the possibility of low income in a poor location, during holiday periods, or in slack seasons. Public stenography demands a high degree of skill and flexibility, too, for each new dictator is new, with unique demands and requirements.

PROFESSIONAL ORGANIZATIONS IN THE SECRETARIAL FIELD

The largest professional organization for secretaries is Professional Secretaries International (PSI), a nonprofit association, which has a membership of more than 40,000 secretaries throughout the world. It "promotes competence and recognition of the profession and represents interests and welfare of persons working in and preparing for secretarial and related positions." This organization holds meetings and workshops at the local, state, and national levels, which are planned to improve the secretarial performance of its members. It sponsors a future secretaries association program, mostly at the high school level, to inform students about the secretarial profession and to interest them in entering the field.

In addition, PSI is responsible for the Certified Professional Secretaries (CPS) program, which is an effort to distinguish top-level secretaries from so-called "secretaries." Each year, the Institute for Certifying Secretaries administers a two-day examination in six areas. It is administered in business in centers located in the United States, Virgin Islands, Canada, Puerto Rico, and Malaysia. Nationalized versions are given in Jamaica and Canada. The areas covered by the examination are: behavioral science in business, business law, economics and management, accounting, office administration and communication, and office technology.

Information about the CPS examination may be obtained from the Institute for Certifying Secretaries, a department of Professional Secretaries International, 301 East Armour Boulevard, Kansas City, MO 64111-1299.

The examination is primarily for qualified, experienced secretaries, but students enrolled in two- or four-year colleges may take the examination during their last year. Even if they pass the examination, however, they may not be certified as CPSs until they have acquired four or two years of secretarial experience, respectively.

Since the first CPS examination in 1951, almost 20,000 secretaries have been certified. Because of the difficulty of the examination, secretaries devote many hours or even years to preparation. The program's contribution to management in improved secretarial performance is incalculable. Some colleges give credit for passing the examination and encourage CPSs to complete their formal education. Many corporations give some form of recognition to the secretaries when they pass the examination, such as a one-grade promotion or an automatic salary increase.

Legal secretaries are eligible for membership in the National Association of Legal Secretaries (International), which also sponsors a professional examination and certification program. Educational secretaries may belong to the National Association of Educational Secretaries, a department of the National Education Association with offices in Washington, D.C. This group works for improvement of salaries, retirement benefits, and tenure coverage for its members. It also sponsors a professional standards program designed to upgrade the profession.

CHAPTER 5

INFORMATION/WORD PROCESSING

Information is the basic resource of any company. It takes many forms, including text (letters, memorandum, reports), data (figures), images, and voice. The foundation of information processing is *word-processing,* a concept which fostered the growth of office automation. Word processing has opened up many challenging job opportunities and exciting career paths. This chapter will familiarize you with the automated office environment as it evolved and expanded into a total systems concept.

Although words have been processed ever since paper was produced, the term *word processing* (WP) was adopted to describe a concept that improved the efficiency of inputting, processing, storing, and distributing business communications. Word processing began with the introduction of the Magnetic Tape Selectric Typewriter (MT/ST), the first text-editing typewriter, which could capture keystrokes, could record them on magnetic tape, and could retrieve them for automatic playback. That led to the development of a wide array of dedicated word processors, to a systems approach for office procedures, to a reorganization of office personnel, and to a clearly defined structure for careers paths. Because of the high cost of each word processor and the expensive service contracts, it was not feasible to place a machine near each secretary. Therefore, large word processing centers were organized to process the documents for the entire company. It became apparent that this structure did not serve the needs of all companies, and gradually some companies moved toward decentralization or satellite centers, which are located near the user departments. The number of these decentralized areas, or satellite clusters, as they are often referred to, varies according to the size and needs of the company. Within these areas, specially trained operators spend their entire working day producing printed output (hardcopy). In effect, in these centers, words are processed in much the same way that numbers are processed in data processing centers.

In recent years, microcomputers, which were once used exclusively for processing data, have been purchased for word processing centers as well as for individual work stations of secretarial staff and executives. The word processing software has the same options that can be performed on word processing equipment. Among the remarkable and vast capabilities of each category of equipment are the abilities to display corrected copy on a screen in front of an operator, to move copy from one position to another, to search for data, to merge materials from several sources to produce one document, to produce lists of information such as names and addresses, to sort information, and to verify mathematical calculations. With some software packages, microcomputers with adequate memory can perform graphics, telecommunications, and spreadsheet applications. Now, in addition to text and data, graphs, charts, and columnar work can be performed and integrated in the output. The microcomputer is highly versatile and that, in conjunction with the moderate cost, makes it a valuable tool. It is also possible to send material from one word processing center to a distant company location by computer, thus saving delivery time and expense in preparing a hardcopy output.

ORGANIZATION OF A WORD PROCESSING CENTER

Organizational patterns and job titles have not been standardized in word processing centers, for each company designs its center to serve its individual needs. When the concept of word processing centers first became a reality, the structure was meant for specialized workers whose sole jobs were to operate equipment.

118　Opportunities in Office Occupations

Some organizations also organized centralized administrative support centers. The administrative center never reached the growth potential forecasted, and some centers have even disappeared. However, to compensate, some word processing centers have a more flexible structure that includes administrative support personnel. The number of administrative secretaries depends on the needs of the group and the number of principals the center serves. This position might be strictly administrative and include functions in which the secretary excels, such as records management or library research; or it might include operating a computer. The flow charts that follow are only two possible setups. Chart 10 illustrates the reorganization of functions when a word processing center is established; it illustrates the interrelationships of word processing and administrative support procedures.

In this plan, the administrative secretary (administrative-support secretary) gets materials ready for dictation, and the principal dictates (may be the administrative secretary if the material is routine). In this word processing unit there are four components: the receiving station, which logs in the received dictation; the word processing manager, who decides the order in which the work is to be done and assigns the work to the individual operators; the correspondence secretary (sometimes called word processor) who operates the power equipment; and the center coordinator, who proofreads the transcripts. The approved transcripts are then sent back to the administrative secretary, who attaches the necessary enclosures and approves the document for signing. The principal signs, and the administrative secretary distributes the output.

Chart 11 shows one actual organization plan for the word processing center in a large firm.

This center operates both day and night to ensure maximum use of its equipment. The word processing manager has full responsibility for both day and night operations; the coordinator-scheduler sees that there is an even flow of work to the word processors. Because there have been serious problems with the quality of work produced in this particular center, two proofreader-

CHART 10
Reorganization of Functions When a Word Processing Center is Established

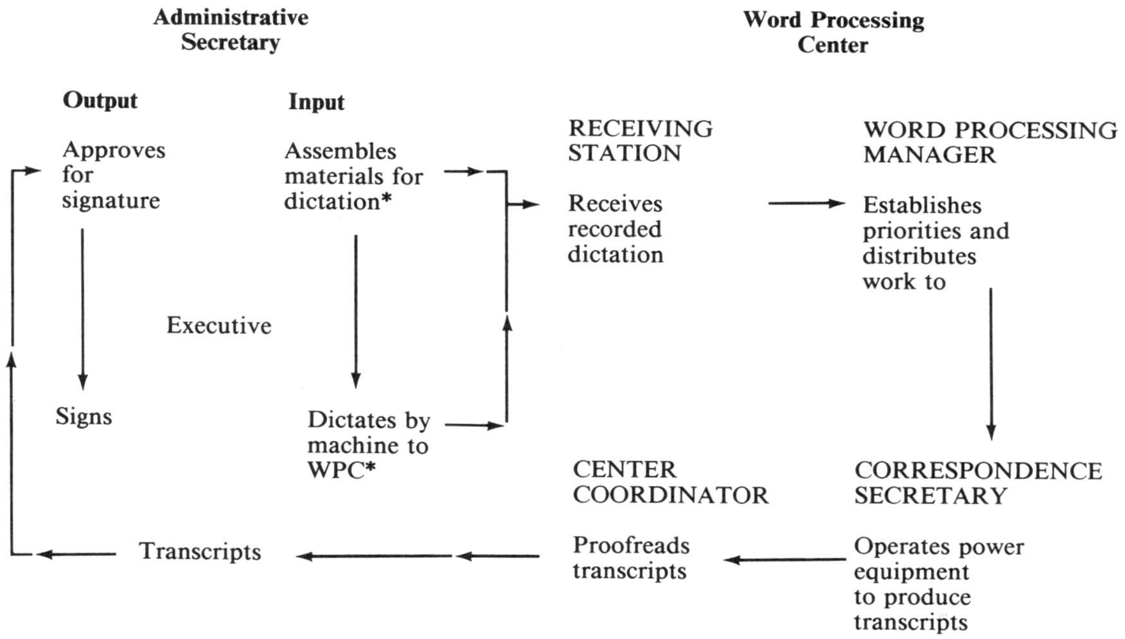

Administrative Secretary

Output	Input
Approves for signature	Assembles materials for dictation*
Executive	
Signs	Dictates by machine to WPC*
Transcripts	

Word Processing Center

- **RECEIVING STATION** — Receives recorded dictation
- **WORD PROCESSING MANAGER** — Establishes priorities and distributes work to
- **CORRESPONDENCE SECRETARY** — Operates power equipment to produce transcripts
- **CENTER COORDINATOR** — Proofreads transcripts

*the administrative secretary may also be the originator of dictation.

CHART 11
Organization Plan for a Word Processing Center

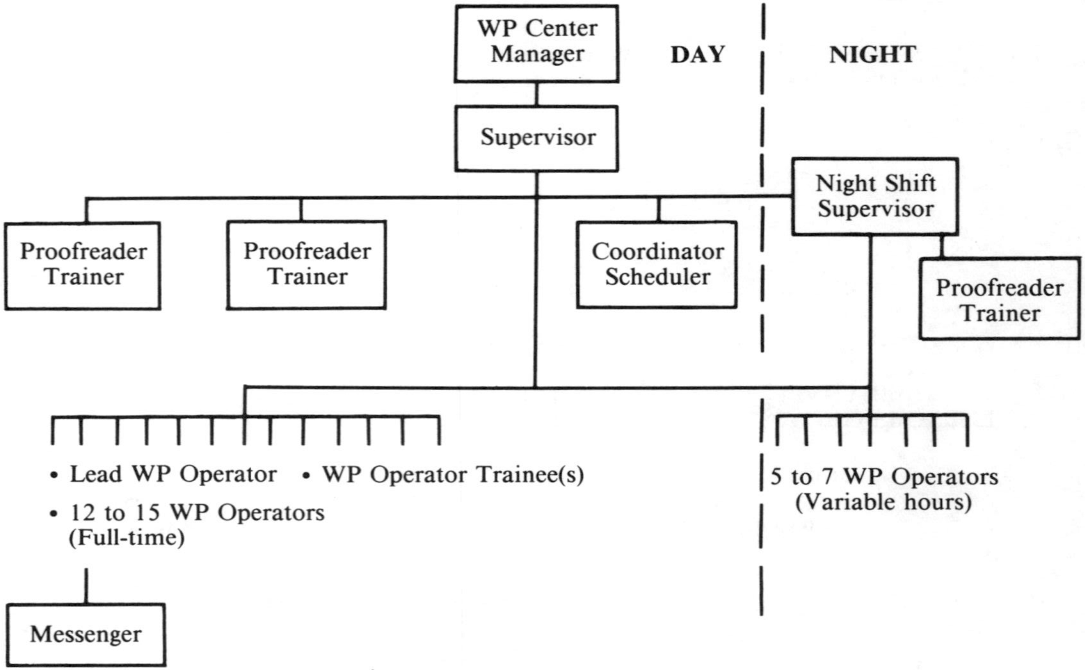

```
                    WP Center Manager
                         |
                      Supervisor
       _____|_____
       |                 |                |                |
  Proofreader      Proofreader      Coordinator       Night Shift
   Trainer          Trainer          Scheduler        Supervisor
                                                          |
                                                     Proofreader
                                                       Trainer
```

DAY | NIGHT

Day shift operators:
- Lead WP Operator • WP Operator Trainee(s)
- 12 to 15 WP Operators (Full-time)

Night shift operators:
- 5 to 7 WP Operators (Variable hours)

Messenger

trainers are required to check the work of the 12 to 15 correspondence secretaries and to train them to make fewer errors. Because it takes at least six months for a new employee to reach full production capability, trainees are being prepared for permanent assignment all of the time.

SKILL REQUIREMENTS AND DUTIES OF PERSONNEL IN WORD PROCESSING CENTERS

Each center is unique and assigns job titles differently. A person who operates a computer or word processor might be designated as a word processing operator in one center, as a correspondence secretary in another, and as a Wang specialist in still another. General skill requirements include good keyboarding skills; a thorough knowledge of the rules of spelling, English grammar, and punctuation; a knowledge of proper formatting of correspondence; and the ability to transcribe from dictated material. In addition to these requirements, the administrative secretary who also uses equipment should have good communication skills. Below are typical job titles and brief descriptions of the positions.

Word Processor or Correspondence Secretary. This operator transcribes dictation from voicewriting equipment, keyboarding as rapidly as possible and correcting errors automatically. Sometimes the dictator wants only a rough draft so that corrections and changes can be made before a final copy is prepared. Most of the time, though, the keyboarded material is played out into a usable document.

The word processor is responsible, too, for playing back stored text when the same material is needed again. The whole document may be reproduced, or portions of different stored transcripts may be merged into new output.

The operator must have, to an exceptional degree, the same first qualification required of a traditional secretary—an understanding of words and their correct usage in business communication. Since dictation is from a remote station, there is no opportunity to ask about terms, and the operator cannot make sensible transcripts without a thorough understanding of the business referred to in the dictation. This means that a topnotch word processor must be a highly intelligent person who knows a great deal about the organization's operations. Finally, a word processor must be interested in mechanical equipment and must understand its capabilities.

Proofreader-Trainer. A word processor who is superior in English mechanics and who displays the communications skills necessary for teaching would normally be promoted to proofreader-trainer.

Scheduler or Logger. The employee who schedules the work of the word processors is a specialized clerk. Some of the items noted on the control sheet prepared in this job are: an assigned number for the job; the nature of the dictation (report, table, instructions, or contract, for instance); nature of the copy (cassette, handwritten copy, rough draft); quality required in output (rough draft or final copy); stationery required; storage; length of storage (temporary or permanent); word processor to whom job is assigned; starting time; finishing time; number of pages; and time of logging out. To maintain this record, the clerk must not only like detail and be meticulous in accuracy but also be able to make decisions about the output. Another important qualification is the ability to delegate the work of the word processors so that each person does a fair share.

Supervisor. Supervisory jobs require the same competencies needed by anyone responsible for the performance of other workers. They delegate, coordinate, and schedule activities; devise, recommend, and implement procedural changes; and prepare performance appraisals. They are above the clerical classification; however, they are a possible promotion channel for the word processor.

THE INFORMATION PROCESSING SPECIALIST

In "Information Processing Specialist: A Redefinition of the Administrative Support Function," Margaret S. Kirby and J. Dale

Oliver report the findings from a study in Virginia of the task analysis of three categories of administrative support workers (supervisor of word processing, secretary, and information processing specialist) who use information/word processing equipment and related technology. The study revealed that word processing and related electronic technology have impacted the way in which office tasks are performed. The data indicated that:

- Eighty-seven percent of the respondents use a dedicated or standalone word processor, while only 10 percent reported using a microcomputer;
- Word processing equipment is being used increasingly in decentralized locations by secretaries;
- The primary source of document input was from longhand (89 percent) and almost two-thirds (63 percent) inputted from machine transcription;
- Documents are inputted from shorthand by 27 percent of all respondents compared to 45 percent by the secretaries;
- Administrative support workers use word processing equipment that is interfaced with printers and electronic communications systems.

In addition to the usual duties of preparing correspondence, collating, printing, proofreading, and handling the telephone, tasks performed by at least 50 percent of the information processing specialists/word processors include:

- Facilitating hardware repair and maintenance*
- Establishing work priorities for information/word processing*
- Initializing diskettes*
- Keyboarding documents from machine transcription, longhand, and rough draft
- Preparing mailing labels and envelopes*
- Preparing and maintaining backup files*
- Storing repetitive (boilerplate) materials
- Moving, rearranging, searching, and replacing text
- Renaming files*
- Preparing new documents from existing documents*
- Maintaining magnetic media

- Copying one disk to another

Tasks performed by approximately 50 percent of the secretaries are those items that have an asterisk above in addition to the following:

- Composing correspondence and other communications
- Keyboarding documents from longhand and rough draft
- Maintaining filing system (nonelectronic)
- Maintaining appointment calendar
- Making travel arrangements and reservations
- Distributing mail
- Preparing correspondence and documents for mailing

The gap between types of tasks performed by secretaries, word processors, and information processing specialists is narrowing as the previous data indicate. Thus, a redefinition of the administrative support function is in order.

REACTIONS OF MANAGEMENT TO WORD PROCESSING

Management no longer has to be sold on the concept of word processing. The cost-cutting features, quick turnaround time, and immediate access to stored information are just a few reasons for the growth of word processing. One company reports that production has doubled with word processing—from 250–300 lines a day previously produced by typists at individual work stations to 500–800 lines a day by correspondence secretaries.

Management also is happy with word processing systems because they allow secretarial output to be measured. Under the traditional system, the only supervisor of output was the executive for whom the secretary worked; most executives were neither trained in nor especially interested in work measurement. Now, the word processing center is manned by someone who does know how to apply quality and quantity measurement standards.

Still, some executives, who regard secretaries as status symbols, resist reorganization of the secretarial function. They dislike dictating to a machine.

In "A Portrait of WP in Transition," Donald D. Bentley writes that the word processing center is becoming an "endangered species" or, at best, a "moving target." He suggests that word processing managers and supervisors, when asked if the word processing center should be disbanded, should be prepared to respond to questions on the role of the center, scope of operations, and staffing. The following comments are considerations in planning a word processing center.

> "Work stations are required for electronic mail, decision support, and database management; it makes sense to use the word processing capabilities."
>
> "The most important application for which microcomputers are being used are word processing applications."
>
> "The ability to integrate text with graphics, to distribute it electronically, and to output typeset-quality material from laser printers is a powerful consideration for a center."
>
> "Since the microcomputer has revolutionized the office, typewriters should be replaced with microcomputers or terminals."
>
> "The four dimensions of the role of manager include managing personnel, satisfying users, satisfying management, and dealing with the office automation community."

REACTIONS OF SECRETARIES TO WORD PROCESSING

The traditional secretary treasures a close relationship with top management. To be successful, he or she must have a personality that meshes with that of the principal. The secretary's status depends on the job title of the principal, not upon objective evaluation of his or her work. A secretary who is established in the executive suite is not likely to covet the word processor's job. However, personal computers are being placed at the disposal of secretaries. Thus, they are being mainstreamed into word processing systems. Secretaries may coordinate with the word processing centers for the more routine, repetitive work and large multiple-page jobs, while they perform the daily correspondence and the rush and confidential tasks.

More and more secretaries, though, welcome the freedom from

routine that automated typing brings and the time that is freed for more challenging jobs. Some of them opt for jobs in word processing centers. They enjoy the opportunities such positions offer for producing larger volumes of higher quality documents, and they like the idea of being word and information specialists. Others are attracted strictly to the duties of an administrative group. Although administrative secretaries realize that they have to adjust to the whims of several bosses rather than just one, they see their opportunities for promotion increased in direct proportion to the number of principals they serve. They also perceive the career paths available within the centers themselves whenever they develop their supervisory and administrative skills.

A Kelly Services study of 507 secretaries employed by major companies in the United States was conducted to determine the impact of word processing on job functions and attitudes of secretaries. The findings show that secretaries are overwhelmingly happy with word processing (83 percent), that the overall number of secretaries employed in the companies with word processing equipment (approximately 70 percent) remained on the job, that secretaries with word processing skills have a higher status than those without skills (approximately 50 percent), that electronic equipment has opened up new opportunities for secretaries (60 percent), that the word processor has reduced typing time so that secretaries have more time to do work that involves responsibility and decision making, and that the younger secretaries are most fully integrated into the electronic office and more likely to spend the bulk of their week operating word processing equipment.

Most important of all, the office worker of tomorrow must be flexible and ready to accept change. Word processing is bringing the kind of dramatic change that data processing triggered in the past.

Anyone now in an office job or preparing for one must accept change and must be able to adjust to it. In fact, the areas in which changes are occurring are the areas in which the greatest opportunities lie.

SALARIES

Salaries of word processors are slightly lower than those of secretaries. A review of the 1986 *Office Salaries Report* of the Administrative Management Society reveals that the average weekly salary in 1986 of a word processing operator, level A, $302, was below that of a secretary, level A, and an accounting clerk, level A. A lead word processing operator, however, receives an average weekly salary of $349, which is above that of a secretary, Level A, and an accounting clerk, Level A, but below that of a legal secretary/assistant and an executive secretary/administrative assistant. Salaries are rising, as reflected in a comparison of 1985 and 1986 statistics, with the exception of word processing operator, level B, which shows a seven-tenths percent drop. The largest increase has been for the clerk typist, whose salary increased 5 percent from $241 in 1985 to $253 in 1986, followed by the executive secretary/administrative assistant, whose salary increased from $368 to $384. (See Chart 12.)

IS SHORTHAND ON THE WAY OUT?

"Gregg shorthand is a dying skill," states Charlotte Low in "Shorthand's Fading Mark." In the last issue of this book, a news release from the International Information/Word Processing Association indicated that "Shorthand skill was becoming an archaic job requirement." Supporting data from surveys and individuals of repute in industry were given to refute these statements. It is now six years later, and the debate about the need for shorthand is still going on.

Some of the reasons Low gives for the demise of shorthand are: rising use of dictating machines, decreased demand for high speeds, and about 3 percent of the working members of the National Shorthand Reporters Association write by hand. Other supportive data from research on the decreasing demand for shorthand skills show that in one study, reported by Kay Fusselman in "Job Market for Secretaries Exceptionally Strong," only 20 percent of employers seeking permanent office help asked for short-

128   *Opportunities in Office Occupations*

hand, compared with 35 percent in 1985. In another study, opinions about the importance of shorthand depend upon the age of the respondents. Only 17 percent of the 18- to 24-year age group considered it important, compared with 20 percent of those 25- to 34-years old, 26 percent of those 35- to 49-years old, and 33 percent of those aged 50 and over. Overall, only one in five secretaries, or 22 percent, gave shorthand a top rating for importance, according to the Kelly Report. Apparently, the more mature age group values the shorthand skills more than younger people. In her previously cited discussion of the role of secretaries, Angela Angerosa points out that dictation/transcription machines have made shorthand all but obsolete.

CHART 12
Office Salaries
1985–1986

Title	1985	1986	% Change
Word Processing			
Lead Word Processing Operator	$335	$349	4.2
Word Processor Level A	300	302	0.7
Word Processor Level B	271	269	–0.7
Secretarial			
Executive Secretary/ Administrative Assistant	368	384	4.3
Legal Secretary/Assistant	—	365	—
Secretary Level A	316	328	3.8
Secretary Level B	283	289	2.1
Accounting			
Accounting Clerk Level A	317	323	1.9
Payroll Clerk	307	318	3.6
General Clerical			
Clerk Typist	241	253	5.0

Based on 1986 *Office Salaries Report*, Administrative Management Society

Findings from two other studies give a different viewpoint, however. The Professional Secretaries International Research and Educational Foundation sponsored a survey of the 1988 newspaper help-wanted advertisements, cited in Fusselman's article. The percentage of ads requesting shorthand, fast notetaking, or secretarial skills (which implies shorthand) was only 20.3 percent compared to 22.6 percent in 1987, 26.1 percent in 1986, and 33 percent in 1985. However, the percentage of ads requesting shorthand for the executive secretary was 51.5 percent, compared to 47.7 percent in 1987. Apparently, there is still a demand for shorthand in upper-level positions. In the New York City metropolitan area, the Shorthand Teachers' Association of the Business Education Association of Metropolitan New York conducted a survey of 200 companies to determine the status of shorthand. More than half, or 52 percent, of the respondents require shorthand for entry-level secretarial positions and 64 percent for promotion. Currently, businesses also have available an average of 23 positions that require shorthand per company; however a decrease in demand is anticipated, according to Avis O. Anderson and Audrey Harrigan in "Investigation of the Status of Shorthand in Business and Education."

Proponents of shorthand rationalize the need for its usefulness. In terms of salary, shorthand is worth between $100 and $200 a month. Administrative secretaries can save time and be more productive. Secretaries who dictate to word processing centers can organize their ideas for the dictation into logical sequence by making shorthand notes. Letters that are thought through carefully come back in usable form rather than in rough draft.

Administrative secretaries can save time, too, in researching material for reports, in drafting procedures, or in abstracting material if they can make shorthand notes. If they make notes during interviews with other company personnel, they can provide themselves, and often their principals, with exact records. They can take notes in shorthand during meetings and later prepare typewritten proceedings of a conference or a committee meeting. The proceedings or minutes will be available faster if they use shorthand than if they have to listen to a complete recording. Obviously, shorthand is indispensable for recording telephone conversations, whether the secretary is monitoring a conversation between a principal and an outside caller or is simply taking a message. A final argument for learning shorthand is the advantage it gives the administrative secretary who decides to change jobs. It is often the ace up the sleeve that makes the difference.

Is the demise of shorthand in the foreseeable future? It might be because there is a whole new mix of office employees whose primary language is not English. Therefore, they cannot master shorthand and transcription. A very apparent need is English, according to Richard W. Stevenson in "Employers Teaching English to Their Immigrant Workers." That *is* in demand!

CHAPTER 6
THE BOOKKEEPER-ACCOUNTANT

A financial recordkeeping system is vital to the successful functioning of an organization, and business needs up-to-date records for wise decision making. These records are maintained in journals, ledgers, and computer memories by bookkeepers and accounting clerks, a term used synonymously with bookkeepers by the government.

Reliable sources of data are the lifeblood of business that must gather, process, distribute, utilize, and store information. The variety of procedures used to process the data range from the simple hand method to electromechanical and electronic methods. Automated equipment and the increasing volume of business have given rise to new job titles for people who process data, such as accountant, auditor, key entry operator, computer machine operator, systems analyst, and programmer. In each category, there are lines of demarcation reflecting different levels of skills and education as well as specialization of tasks. Chapters 6 and 7 give an overview of this occupational field.

Recent statistics show that over 2.1 million workers are engaged in bookkeeping activities with another 945,000 employed as accountants. (See Chart 13.) Although the anticipated increase in employment for bookkeepers by the year 2000 is only 4 percent, mainly due to computerization of functions, job openings will be numerous because the occupation is so large. As the number of businesses increases, so will the demand for accountants who will be needed to set up books, prepare taxes, give management advice, and provide information about accounting records and procedures.

CHART 13
Number of Bookkeeping and Accounting Employees
1986–2000

Job Title	1986	2000	Percent Growth 1986–2000
		(Projected)	
Accounting Clerks and Bookkeepers	2,116,000	2,208,000	4.0
Accountants and Auditors	945,000	1,321,000	40.0

Based on data from Department of Labor.

Bookkeeping jobs are found in every type and size of business, including law firms, insurance companies, and banks. Bookkeepers also work in schools, hospitals, factories, and government agencies. The data reflect that approximately one bookkeeper out of three works for a retail or wholesale firm, and approximately one-quarter of all of the bookkeepers and accounting clerks work part-time. In banks, bookkeepers are the largest single group of clerks.

In the business of yesteryear (and even in some small offices today), a general bookkeeper kept the entire set of books—from journal to balance sheet to profit-and-loss statement. This bookkeeper would analyze and record all financial transactions, balance the accounts, and prepare invoices and payrolls. However, as businesses changed from small, single proprietorships to corporations, the tasks usually performed by the one bookkeeper are divided among many workers.

In large businesses, the bookkeepers and accounting clerks specialize and work under a head bookkeeper or accountant. A bookkeeping staff may include a number of specialized clerical workers:

- Entry clerk, who enters charge sales and credits

allowances;
- Billing clerk, who compiles and prepares customer charges and ascertains from computer printouts monthly costs, amount of work completed, and type of work performed for customers. Operates a calculator and typewriter;
- Invoicing systems operator, who works in the accounting office and who uses a computer terminal to prepare billing invoices and to generate statements, such as daily sales and commissions; handles order packing lists;
- Inventory clerk, who compiles records of merchandise and maintains an updated inventory;
- Payroll clerk, who handles personnel payroll;
- Accounts payable clerk, whose sole concern is with company purchases.

The job title "bookkeeper," causes confusion because it may describe the clerk performing a specific limited bookkeeping function or it may describe a bookkeeper responsible for a complete set of books. The *Dictionary of Occupational Titles* defines bookkeeping jobs as a group of "occupations concerned with computing, classifying, and recording numerical data to keep sets of financial records complete." The job descriptions for the two categories of bookkeepers follow:

Bookkeeper I (full-charge or general). Keeps records of financial transactions of establishment. Verifies and enters details of transactions as they occur or in chronological order in account and cash journals from items such as sales slips, invoices, check stubs, inventory records, and requisitions. Summarizes details on separate ledgers, using adding machine, and transfers data to general ledger. Balances books and compiles reports to show statistics, such as cash receipts and expenditures, accounts payable and receivable, profit and loss, and other items pertinent to operation of business. Calculates employee wages from plant records or timecards and makes up checks or withdraws cash from bank for payment of wages. May prepare withholding, social security, and other tax reports. May compute, type, and mail monthly statements to customers. May complete books to or through trial balance. May operate calculating and bookkeeping machine.

Bookkeeper II. Keeps one section of set of financial records, performing duties as described under Bookkeeper I. May be designated according to section of bookkeeping records kept, such as accounts-payable bookkeeper; accounts-receivable bookkeeper; Christmas-Club bookkeeper (banking); interest-accrual bookkeeper (banking); safe-deposit bookkeeper (banking); savings bookkeeper (banking).

Also employed in this category are the accounting clerks, as indicated at the beginning of this chapter. The accounting clerk primarily performs the routine accounting clerical operations of posting and verifying as well as preparing journal vouchers. The job descriptions for the levels of accounting clerks are:

Accounting Clerk. Performs one or more accounting tasks, such as posting to registers and ledgers; balancing and reconciling accounts; verifying the internal consistency, completeness, and mathematical accuracy of accounting documents; assigning prescribed accounting distribution codes; examining and verifying the clerical accuracy of various types of reports, lists, calculations, postings etc.; preparing journal vouchers; or making entries or adjustments to accounts.

An accounting clerk I performs simple, routine accounting clerical operations and receives clear and detailed instructions for specific assignments from the supervisor. Work is closely reviewed for accuracy. An accounting clerk II performs one or more routine accounting clerical operations, such as examining, verifying, and correcting accounting transactions to ensure completeness and accuracy of data. Completed work is reviewed for accuracy and compliance with procedures. Levels III and IV require a knowledge and understanding of the established and standardized bookkeeping and accounting procedures and techniques used in an accounting system, or a segment of an accounting system, where there are few variations in the types of transactions handled. In addition, some jobs at each level may require a basic knowledge and understanding of the terminology, codes, and processes used in an automated accounting system.

The question naturally arises at this point as to the difference between a bookkeeper and an accountant. Basically, the difference between the two centers around the exercise of judgment. The work of a bookkeeper is confined largely to making routine entries in accounting records, without the need of a knowledge of accounting or the exercise of judgment. An accountant, on the other hand, is required to exercise sound judgment in his or her work. This judgment is based on a sound knowledge of accounting principles and techniques. Accountants are responsible for devising systems and procedures so that the financial affairs of organizations can be recorded and translated into meaningful financial statements. They must be able to interpret the accumulated data recorded in the organization's books so that proper policy decisions can be made.

In no other clerical field has the increase in the employment of women been so pronounced as in the bookkeeping area. From a completely masculine personnel, the change has been so great that today over 90 percent of the bookkeepers are women. Increasing numbers of women also are entering the professional field of accounting.

EDUCATIONAL REQUIREMENTS AND PERSONAL APTITUDES

Computer literacy is important for the individual interested in accounting as a career not only to learn how to perform routine accounting tasks, such as making journal entries and posting, but also to be able to access data banks. However, learning how to perform these operations is inadequate unless it is coupled with an understanding of the basic accounting principles. The ability to analyze a transaction, to see relationships between what is recorded and the final products that are generated, and to recognize errors will help ensure successful careers in accounting. Dr. Ginger Rose believes that individuals on the high school level will understand the process if they can do the following:

- Apply the rules of debiting and crediting with an understanding of the "why" rather than memorization of a procedure;
- Analyze business transactions in terms of their effect on the accounting equation (Assets equals Liabilities + Owner's Equity) through all steps of the accounting cycle;
- Perform manually all the steps of the accounting cycle;
- Use the General Journal for manual input of cash receipts, cash payments, purchases, sales, personnel and payroll, and general accounting, followed up by viewing the individual tasks as a comprehensive system;
- Handle integrated computer projects.

Individual who are planning a career in accounting should have an analytical mind, an aptitude for mathematics, an ability to use good judgment based on knowledge, the expertise to communicate both orally and in writing, the ability to concentrate, and the ability to assume responsibility with a minimum of supervision.

EDUCATIONAL PREPARATION

In choosing workers for bookkeeping jobs, most employers hire people who have completed high school. In coming years, however, many of the jobs opening up in automated offices will require education beyond high school.

Most large high schools have an accounting concentration in their business and marketing departments, which would be available for students interested in vocational preparation for this field. In addition to required courses in English, science, math, and social studies, a student would have to take the core courses in business plus several units from the following list: basic accounting, advanced accounting, college accounting, business analysis/business computer applications, electronic information processing, principles of marketing, and financial information processing. Some topics students would study in the core courses would be personal management, economic concepts, decision making, and careers.

Community colleges offer accounting specializations that prepare graduates to enter positions as bookkeepers, cost accounting clerks, and junior accountants. Principles of finance, economics, and introductory courses in data processing also are included in the curriculum.

Schools strive constantly to update their bookkeeping and accounting training programs to keep pace with the current trends in the job market. Traditionally, during the first year of training, stress is placed on the mastery of journalizing, posting, and trial balance components.

Students might complete training modules dealing with a service business, with specialized journals appropriate to a mercantile business, with principal bookkeeping subsystems that might be found in a multiple-bookkeeper establishment, or with simulated tasks performed by entry-level bookkeepers such as payroll clerk, accounts receivable clerk, and accounts payable clerk.

THE BOOKKEEPER IN THE AUTOMATED OFFICE

The duties of many bookkeepers are likely to change considerably as more firms make use of electronic computers and accounting and recordkeeping software applications. Nevertheless, a thorough knowledge of basic accounting procedures is still an absolute necessity. Another very important qualification of the bookkeeper is an aptitude for working with figures and for concentrating on detail.

The use of computers to automate the bookkeeping/accounting process has contributed to simplifying tasks that were once tedious and time-consuming to perform. With appropriate software, postings can be handled automatically and accurate financial records can be maintained. No longer need statements and payrolls be done manually for they can be generated automatically from the machine. Since all types of businesses are automating their accounting operations, the person interested in a career in this field should be familiar with the use of accounting software applications in addition to an understanding of the accounting process.

HOW TO GET STARTED

Beginning bookkeepers use the same sources of employment as other applicants for positions in the clerical field: the high school or college placement office, the state employment service, newspaper advertisements, suggestions of friends. They are interviewed by a representative of the personnel department and are later sent for an interview to the department in which the vacancy exists.

Clerical ability tests may be administered, or specific bookkeeping tests may be given. Candidates may be given a set of books containing entries already partially made; they continue entering the transactions in the proper manner and obtain certain interpretive data from the journals—just as they would continue the work of their predecessors if they took the position.

Many students who have taken part in cooperative programs while in school may find permanent positions in the firms in which they worked as students.

THE WORKING SITUATION FOR THE BOOKKEEPER

The bookkeeper should have good eyesight, for eyestrain is the principal hazard of the job. Bookkeepers should develop accurate and legible handwriting and should have manual dexterity and good coordination of eye and hand movements. The hours and conditions of work are similar to those found in other clerical occupations. The work is done in clean surroundings, and good working conditions generally prevail. Along with other office workers, bookkeepers receive fringe benefits such as health insurance and retirement pensions.

Bookkeeping positions provide a worker with the chance to learn the details of business operations. With so much of the work being done on automated equipment, however, it is extremely likely that each bookkeeping employee will be handling only one, or a few, of the many kinds of work necessary to keep a complete set of books. Thus, it may not always be possible to learn the overall picture necessary for complete understanding.

The greatest disadvantage of bookkeeping work, especially in the lower positions, is its lack of variety and its monotony. The extreme specialization in the special bookkeeper's job makes the work routine in nature and definitely unchallenging.

SALARIES

Salary statistics for 1986 compiled by the U.S. Bureau of Labor Statistics revealed that accounting clerks do well. The monthly salaries ranged from $1,043–1,823. On the average, the beginning salary was higher than that paid to beginning file clerks but less than beginning secretaries or stenographers. Experienced accounting clerks in level IV earned more than comparable level file clerks and typists; however, the salary was less than a level IV secretary. Interestingly, an accounting clerk at level IV earns $71 per month more than a beginning accountant. It is important to mention, however, that an accountant's salary reaches $3,274 per month at level IV and goes as high as $5,129 on the top level. A look at civil service figures, according to a 1984 survey by the International Personnel Management Association showed that the average beginning salary for accounting clerks at all levels of government positions was $12,636 a year; for experienced workers it was $16,248. In 1985, an accounting clerk in the federal government with two years of experience or postsecondary education received a starting salary of $12,862 a year. Those figures can be compared to a 1985 survey of private industry by the Administrative Management Society, which showed that entry-level accounting clerks averaged $13,832, while accounting clerks with more responsibility earned $16,484. Experienced bookkeepers earned an annual average salary of $17,264 in 1985. Clearly, the salaries were higher in private industry.

Salaries for accounting clerks vary by industry and tend to be higher in public utilities and mining and lowest in finance, insurance, and real estate.

ACCOUNTING CAREERS

The normal promotion channel for a bookkeeping employee would be from a general bookkeeper or accounting clerk to head bookkeeper or accountant. The climb upward within the company, however, is rather slow. The top jobs in the recordkeeping field usually go to trained accountants who qualify on the professional level. Most important for an accountant, no matter what the specialty, is to gain computer skills. Learn to use some of the basic systems, for this will be an asset during your career.

The highest level of professional skill that may be achieved in accountancy is recognized by a certificate designating the holder as a CPA (Certified Public Accountant). This certificate ensures the "professional competence of individuals offering their services to the public as professional accountants." To earn it, candidates must meet various state requirements, including the successful completion of a difficult two-and-one-half day written examination. The four sections of the uniform CPA examination are Auditing, Business Law, Accounting Theory, and Accounting Practice, Parts I and II; but a particular state may also require examination in additional subjects such as economics, federal income taxation, government accounting, or ethics. Certified public accountants are the only group of practicing accountants who must demonstrate their competencies by passing the uniform national examination and by meeting other experience qualifications.

Candidates receive credit for the parts of the examination they pass and may retake the sections they fail at a future date. A substantial majority of those who attempt the CPA examination do pass all parts eventually. Awards are presented to candidates who pass all four sections at one time and receive the highest grades. In May 1985, approximately 70,000 candidates took the examination, but only 126 certificates of performance with high distinction were awarded.

Although the CPA certificate originally was intended for public accountants as a means of ensuring high-quality services and ethical standards in work involving a public trust, many people who do not intend to practice public accounting take the CPA examination and obtain a license. It can thus be used as a means of securing promotion to bookkeeping/accounting jobs at the highest levels.

There are about 275,000 CPAs nationally, and although most CPAs are men, women are gaining in importance in public accounting. Women now have their own national professional society, The American Women's Society of Certified Public Accountants.

The majority of states require a bachelor's degree conferred by a college or university that is recognized by the state board of accountancy and an educational program that includes a specified number of credit hours of accounting and related subjects as a prerequisite for taking the CPA examination. The day may not be far off when a college degree will be required in all states. In some states, the educational prerequisite is becoming even more rigid. Florida and Hawaii now mandate five years of education; New York State requires four years of education plus two years of professional experience. A fifth year of education plus one year of experience fulfills the qualifications for candidacy. Many public accounting firms consider only college graduates for positions.

A description of the work of an accountant is given in the *1986–87 Occupational Outlook Handbook* published by the U.S. Department of Labor:

> Managers must have up-to-date financial information to make important decisions. Accountants prepare and analyze and verify financial reports that furnish this kind of information.
>
> Four major accounting fields are public, management, government, and internal auditing. Public accountants are independent practitioners or employees of accounting firms. Management accountants, often called industrial or private accountants, handle the financial records of their firms. Government accountants examine the records of government agencies and audit private busi-

nesses and individuals whose dealings are subject to government regulations.

Accountants often concentrate on one phase of accounting. For example, many public accountants specialize in auditing (examining a client's financial records and reports to judge their compliance with standards of preparation and reporting). Others specialize in tax matters, such as preparing income tax forms and advising clients of the advantages and disadvantages of certain business decisions. Accountants often specialize in management consulting and give advice on a variety of matters. They might develop or revise an accounting system to serve the needs of clients more effectively or give advice about how to manage cash resources more profitably.

TESTING PROGRAM

The American Institute of Certified Public Accountants developed a testing program in an effort to attract qualified young men and women and to provide standards by which their aptitudes could be measured against the demands of a successful accounting career. The tests are made available in three broad service programs known as the college accounting testing program, the professional accounting testing program, and the educational accounting aptitude test.

The educational accounting aptitude test assists beginning college students to determine if they should choose accounting as a profession. The Level I College Achievement Test is a progress check early in the study of accounting. The Level II College Achievement Test aids seniors in finding employment as accountants by making available standardized measurements of aptitude and proficiency for submission to prospective employers. At the professional level, the Professional Accounting Test aids employers in gauging the ability of job applicants and assessing their learning ability. The tests have been used in making decisions regarding retention of temporary workers and in upgrading and promoting permanent staff members.

THE WORKING SITUATION FOR ACCOUNTANTS

Depending on the specialty and type of job, accountants may work long hours and under very heavy pressure during the tax season. Others who are employed by national and international companies may travel extensively to branches to audit the books or to work for clients. The majority of accountants work in urban areas where there is a concentration of businesses.

Increased educational requirements for the profession will probably result so that not only a college education but graduate work will be a normal part of preparation for accounting leadership.

The institute recommends accounting careers to those who are good in mathematics and communication skills and who have the right combination of ability, imagination, and willingness to work in a field with varied and almost unlimited opportunities.

William Hall, retiring partner of Arthur Anderson & Company, stated: "The accountant of today and tomorrow will play a much greater role in business, finance, and government than he did 30 or 40 years ago."

EMPLOYMENT OUTLOOK FOR ACCOUNTANTS

Accounting is one of the fastest-growing professions in the United States because of complex and changing tax systems, pension reform and financial disclosure, growing reliance of executives and managers in large organizations on accounting information to make business decisions, the increasing use of accounting services by small business organizations, the pressure in business and government agencies to improve budgeting and accounting procedures, and insolvencies. In government, accounting is the biggest business of all. Between 1986 and the year 2000, there will be a 40 percent increase in employment, or an increase of 376,000.

The increasing use of computers and the special software systems that have been developed are reducing the amount of tedious work the accountant previously had to perform with figures and records. Thus, accountants have more time for the interpretive aspects of their assignments.

If you are interested in becoming a tax accountant, your first entry-level job might be preparing tax returns. You might work for an accounting company or a firm that specializes in tax service like H & R Block. In general accounting, you might be opening up a set of books, planning budgets, implementing new accounting systems, or working on cost accounting procedures, which involves accounting for every penny spent in the production of a product or service.

The American Institute of Certified Public Accountants predicts a continued rapid growth of the accounting profession in the foreseeable future for the following reasons:

- The need to compete in an international economy, which necessitates more cost controls, studies of management's performance, and more expert help from CPAs in looking ahead;
- The need for more sophisticated accounting data and independent professionals who can take responsibility for its reliability because of more government controls;
- The need to report to the expanding number of investors and creditors the financial condition of a business;
- The need for experts to develop, analyze, interpret, and communicate economic data because of economic, political, and technological developments.

SOURCES OF INFORMATION ABOUT PROFESSIONAL ACCOUNTING CAREERS

- The American Institute of Certified Public Accountants (AICPA), 1211 Avenue of the Americas, New York, NY 10036, is a national society serving more than 265,000 members in public practice in industry, government, and education. The organization provides recruitment materials about the field of accounting. The uniform CPA examination is prepared and graded by the institute and administered by each state. The AICPA library contains the most

The Bookkeeper-Accountant 145

comprehensive collection of accounting materials in the United States. Telephone No. (212) 575-6200.
- National Association of Accountants, 10 Paragon Drive, P.O. Box 433, Montvale, NJ 07645; Telephone No. (201) 574-9000.
- Institute of Internal Auditors, 249 Maitland Avenue, Altamonte Springs, Florida 32701; Telephone No. (305) 830-7600.
- The American Woman's Society of Certified Public Accountants, 111 East Wacker Drive, Suite 600, Chicago, Illinois 60601, was formed in 1933 to promote the interests of qualified women in the field. Telephone No. (312) 644-6610.
- The U.S. Department of Labor publishes data about current employment trends in the field.
- Public accounting is regulated by the state licensing boards, and information about the CPA examinations in each state is available through the state government.

This systems analyst tests a program he has designed. (IBM photo)

CHAPTER 7
PROCESSING DATA BY MACHINE

Data processing (DP) is a method of working with numbers and symbols, and word processing (WP) is concerned with textual material. In data processing, you might be handling customer billing, completing payrolls, recording bank deposits and withdrawals, monitoring factory production processes, or taking and maintaining inventory. In word processing, you would be keyboarding, storing, printing, and distributing office documents such as letters, reports, and memorandums. Initially, when both of these activities (DP and WP) were developed, they were separate and different. In data processing a logical set of instructions was used to carry out functions while with word processing, the operator was involved with manipulation of text. Originally, installations of these two systems were centralized; then gradually they began to decentralize, thus maintaining two structural plans. The trend in data processing was from mainframes to minicomputers to microcomputers and eventually linking up to mainframes by communications lines. In recent years, however, because of the influx of microcomputers, DP and WP are being integrated. This was a logical progression because the traditional applications that were once performed on minicomputers are now being handled on the microcomputers. The most popular applications are word processing, spreadsheets, and database management, according to John W. Verity in "Minis, Micros, and Maturity." This chapter briefly discusses specific data processing careers, employment opportunities, requirements, and qualifications.

A LOOK AT THE TRENDS

Computers are proliferating so rapidly that they have impacted virtually every activity in society. Whether it be at home, in educational institutions, or in the workplace, structural changes have occurred in the ways in which people learn and use information, in the tools used to perform a job, and in the way change is being managed. The electronic data processing system is replacing all other means of processing data and is supplying management with the information it needs to conduct business efficiently.

As new technology is introduced, organizations find more uses for computers, which eventually means a shift and expansion in worker skills. This is inevitable because, as industry experts anticipate in "The Career Planning Cycle: Developing a Sensible Strategy," sales of microcomputers will rise above $300 billion by 1995.

IMPLICATIONS FOR CAREER PLANNING

What are the implications of these trends for the individual looking for employment? First, you must begin to plan your career carefully if you wish to achieve your lifetime goals. Second, you should acquire the basic skills—writing, reading, comprehension, math, and problem solving—which, according to the policy statement of the National Commission for Employment Policy, "will continue to be critical for labor market success, even in the 'computer age.'" (Cited in *Computers in the Workplace: Selected Issues.*) Third, you should realize that computer skills are an addition to the job skills previously required in an occupation.

Machines are just pieces of equipment with artificial intelligence. What is needed are competent, thinking workers at all skill levels who understand the logic of systems and who can design systems, write and maintain software, modify and enhance programs, operate the computers and auxiliary equipment, retrieve results, and maintain systems. The information generated is only as meaningful as the humans that handle the input (the instructions for the computer) and output (the results).

WHERE ELECTRONIC DATA PROCESSING JOBS ARE FOUND

Business is the largest employer of data processing personnel, with the federal government a close second. Typical users are banks, insurance companies, manufacturers of equipment, retail merchandising firms, health care facilities, accounting firms, real estate organizations, and data processing service organizations.

A striking trend of recent years is the use of the small business computer in many areas of everyday life. In the supermarket, the scanner helps the clerk check and bag a product simultaneously; in the hospital, the computer researches and diagnoses a case; in education, computer-assisted instruction individualizes learning; in the government, the Internal Revenue Department evaluates tax returns; and in some courts that are experimenting with computer systems, the computer retrieves data on the criminal status of the defendant, thus assisting the judge in setting bail bonds.

SPECIALIZED DATA PROCESSING JOBS

A glance at the duties of various electronic data processing workers will give you an idea of the specialities available in the field. Job descriptions given in this section are those used by the U.S. Bureau of Labor Statistics. Generally, workers in data processing must be accurate and precise. Other characteristics essential to a successful career in this rapidly changing field are a willingness to learn continuously, to face challenges, and to be flexible and ready to make changes.

Key Entry Operator. Operates keyboard-controlled data entry device such as keypunch machine or key-operated magnetic tape or disc encoder to transcribe data into a form suitable for computer processing. Work requires skill in operating an alphanumeric keyboard and an understanding of transcribing procedures and relevant data entry equipment.

Positions are classified into levels on the basis of the following definitions.

Key Entry Operator I. Performs routine and repetitive tasks under close supervision. Work generally is from standardized and coded source documents. The work of Key Entry Operator II requires experience and judgment.

Computer Operator I. Operates the control console for which on-the-job-training is given, sometimes augmented by classroom training. Works under close supervision with detailed instructions. Computer Operator II processes scheduled routines which present few difficult operating problems and applies standard or corrective procedures to errors in response to computer output instructions or error conditions. A Computer Operator III processes a range of scheduled routines, diagnoses error conditions, and may deviate from standard procedures to find solutions to problems.

Computer Programmer. Writes, and tests the detailed instructions for the machine to follow to organize data, solves problems, and performs other tasks; writes instruction sheets for computer operators; frequently works from descriptions prepared by systems analysts. Applications programmers write software to handle specific jobs, such as inventory control. Systems programmers maintain the software that controls the operation of the entire computer system.

Computer Systems Analyst. Plans and develops methods for computerizing business tasks or improving computer systems already in operation; recommends hardware and software; and designs forms to collect data. The work may involve the design for a system, preparation of charts and diagrams, and doing an analysis for cost justification.

Data Typist/Data Entry Keyer. Uses special machines that convert the information they type to magnetic impulses on tapes or disks, which is then read into the computer. Some keyers operate on-line terminals off the main computer system that transmit and receive data; in small offices, may operate computer peripheral equipment such as printers.

Computer Peripheral and Equipment Operator. Duties vary according to size of installation and firm; in a small installation, may run both computer and all peripheral equipment while in a large computer installation may specialize in console operation or peripheral equipment. Work is generally from operating instructions. They load the equipment with tapes, disks, and paper; monitor the computer console; respond to operating and computer messages; and prepare computer printout.

EDUCATIONAL PREPARATION IN HIGH SCHOOL AND BEYOND

Individuals interested in data processing careers must be trainable and educable so that they can adapt to the technological changes that are occurring at an incredible rate. At the heart of trainability is the ability to read and understand, write and communicate, compute and comprehend one's computations—the most basic of skills—along with the motivation to learn. People preparing to enter the job market, or experienced workers who have these basic skills coupled with computer literacy of varying degrees will have the greatest number of employment opportunities at their disposal. Young people graduating from high school with these skills and abilities will have little difficulty starting an occupation that uses computers. Although a high school diploma is the minimum requirement for entry jobs, a college degree is necessary for higher-level positions such as programmer or systems analyst, where advanced knowledge of computers is necessary. High school graduates will most likely pursue occupations that use standardized computer programs; college graduates are probably more interested in careers requiring more computer-related training—and probably more knowledge of programming. Sources for training are private business schools, computer schools, and company in-house programs.

Specialized data processing courses are offered in the high schools, in occupational centers, in junior and community colleges, and in a number of universities and colleges. Data processing vocabulary and a functional knowledge of various data processing concepts, such as flow charting, are included as units of study in related courses.

The following Sewanahaka High School (Floral Park, New York) occupational requirements for data processing majors (followed by a brief description of the courses) prepares students with the technical skills and general knowledge that will enable them to pursue successful careers in the field.

Grade Level	*Work-bound*	*College-bound*
10th	Business Analysis/Business Computer Applications	Business Analysis/Business Computer Applications
11th	Computer Applications 2	COBOL I
12th	COBOL I	COBOL II

Business Analysis/Business Computer Applications: This course is available to 10th, 11th, or 12 graders. Business Analysis provides students with opportunities to acquire concepts and attitudes essential for understanding and working in business. Its modules are:

COBOL I: This second-level course is for students interested in a computer programming career. It introduces the students to the COBOL programming language. The students use WordStar to enter, compile, and execute their programs on microcomputers. The actual computer operations of programming are performed by each student.

COBOL II: In this third and final year of the data processing program, students acquire an in-depth understanding of computer systems and learn techniques and methods found in businesslike situations. The tasks required in system analysis are covered. Advanced COBOL programming for business applications are taught.

Computer Applications 2: This course is designed for students who do not wish to pursue a career in computer programming. Students will be introduced to the skills required in the business environment for advanced data entry, spreadsheeting, data base management, business graphics, and word processing. Using microcomputers, the students will be provided with hands-on experience that can be applied to future employment.

Chaney and Otto's study "Are Schools Meeting Needs of the Business Community?," investigates secondary and postsecondary schools as well as business firms to determine if the schools were teaching the technological skills and knowledge that business currently require. The study revealed that:

- Ninety-seven percent of the secondary schools offer courses in which the computer is utilized; for example, word processing, data processing, computer literacy. All of the postsecondary schools offer computer-related courses such as introduction to microcomputers and word processing.
- Sixty-seven percent of the secondary schools teach BASIC compared to 47 percent of the postsecondary schools. However, more businesses use COBOL (34 percent) than BASIC (26 percent). More than half of the firms employed computer programmers.
- Both secondary and postsecondary schools reported using a variety of software packages.
- Keyboarding is required for completion of a business program in 54 percent of the secondary schools, compared to 91 percent of the postsecondary schools.
- More than 60 percent of the firms employ data-entry personnel.
- For programming positions, educational and/or experience requirements varied from only a college degree to a degree with programming experience or postsecondary courses plus programming experience.

Based on the above findings, schools within a 250-mile radius of Memphis, Tennessee, are fulfilling the requirements to prepare their students for entry-level computer-oriented jobs.

EMPLOYMENT PROJECTIONS

The forecast looks good for employment of programmers and computer analysts through the year 2000, for it is expected to grow much faster than average as the use of the computer expands. Job prospects will be best for those with a college degree, related experience, and courses in accounting or management. Employment prospects are also good for computer and peripheral equipment operators because of the growth in computer usage. For data-entry keyers, however, employment is expected to decline due to improved data-entry technologies, such as optical scanners, and the growth of direct data-entry techniques, such as the use of computer terminals and storage of data on disks and cassettes.

Below are several reasons for a favorable employment picture through the year 2000:

- About one worker in eight now uses a computer as part of the daily work routine.
- Computers are used as management tools for decision making.
- The organizational demand for computers or computer services is becoming larger.
- There will be continued development of new applications.
- Opportunities are developing with vendors of mini and microcomputers in the areas of software development and programming.
- Computer decentralization in business, which is becoming much more commonplace because of the mini/microcomputers, terminal devices, and communications networks, will increase the need for computer design and support professionals.

As computers become more and more an integral part of business operations, so will computer specialists achieve a level of importance. New hierarchies of career ladders have developed in many firms for computer professionals who have a combination of technical expertise, business knowledge, and foresight.

It is not unusual for these employees to advance in managerial positions.

If you wish to be a programmer or systems analyst, consider the strong growth fields for the coming decade; namely, services, defense, data communications, and artificial intelligence. In services alone, nearly two out of every three computer jobs will occur, especially in software houses (specialists in writing computer programs), consulting firms, and temporary help agencies. Defense-related jobs as programmers and analysts can be obtained through the armed forces, as a civilian in the defense department, or as an employee with a corporation that has defense contracts. In data communications, computer professionals will be needed to connect all equipment—in many firms, the standalone microcomputers to large mainframes. The field of artificial intelligence is expected to grow rapidly during the coming decade. Therefore, an increasing number of jobs will become available.

From 1986–2000, the percentage of change in employment anticipated for data-entry keyers is minus 16 percent; for computer and peripheral equipment operators, a 48 percent increase; for programmers, a 70 percent increase; and for systems analysts, a 76 percent increase. (See Chart 14.)

SALARIES

Chart 15 shows a comparison between the average 1980 and 1986 salaries for selected professional, administrative, technical, and clerical occupations in the United States. A glance at the figures reflects that programmers and systems analysts at the first level earn considerably more than nonsupervisory personnel. At the third level, computer operators III also earn a higher salary than the nonsupervisory personnel, although it is still lower than that earned by programmers and systems analysts.

CHART 14
Employment Projections
1986–2000

Occupation	1986 Employment	Projected 2000 Requirements	Percent Change
Data-Entry Keyer	400,000	334,000	−16.0
Computing & Peripheral Equipment Operator	309,000	457,000	48.0
Programmer	479,000	814,000	70.0
Systems Analyst	331,000	582,000	76.0

Based on data from Bureau of Labor Statistics, Spring 1988

As indicated in a March 1980 wage survey of the United States, the average annual earnings for a key-entry operator I was $9,981 and for a computer operator I, $10,164. Figures for March 1986 indicated a salary for key-entry operator I of $13,146, an increase of 31.7 percent for the period, and for computer operator I, $13,727, an increase of 35.1 percent. (See Chart 15.) Salaries in metropolitan areas are slightly higher than in small cities and rural districts.

The March 1987 national survey was conducted in the service industries. Although these results cannot be directly compared with the data reflected in Chart 15 because jobs in other sectors of the economy were included in these data, a few interesting observations pertaining to salaries can be made. Overall, salaries were lower for key-entry operators I and II, $12,431 and $15,199 respectively; higher for computer operators at level I, $14,067, but lower for levels II, III, and IV, $16,812, $21,020, and $24,673 respectively; approximately the same for computer programmers at levels I and III, $20,980 and $29,435 respectively, but higher for levels II, IV, and V; and lower for systems analysts I, $28,607, but higher for levels II through V.

WOMEN IN DATA PROCESSING CAREERS

Although there is a significant number of women opting for traditional male occupations, the data processing field is still predominantly male. In recent years, more women have been majoring in this field, and the trend will probably continue; however, neither paychecks at all levels nor opportunities for managerial positions have been equalized. A 1984 Source EDP salary survey and a survey of women in information processing positions conducted by The Women in Information Processing (WIP), cited in "How Much $ Do DPers Make?," revealed that only 9 percent of females in corporate management believe women have equal opportunities for moving into top positions in the industry. At beginning levels, women's salaries varied with those of all employees, sometimes slightly higher and other times slightly lower; but the major differences were visible in higher-level positions.

CHART 15
Average Annual Salaries of
Clerical Workers in the United States
1980–1986

	March 1980	March 1986	% Change
Key Entry Operator I	$ 9,981	$13,146	31.71
Key Entry Operator II	11,723	16,901	44.17
Computer Operator I	10,164	13,727	35.05
Computer Operator II	12,016	17,219	43.30
Computer Operator III	12,957	21,524	66.12
Typist I	9,161	12,584	37.37
Typist II	11,010	16,854	53.08
Accounting Clerk I	8,806	12,517	42.14
Accounting Clerk II	10,377	14,687	41.53
File Clerk I	7,889	10,335	31.01
File Clerk II	8,829	12,156	37.68
File Clerk III	11,026	15,625	41.71
Computer Programmer	19,136	20,832	8.87
Systems Analyst	23,244	29,141	25.37

Based on data from the Bureau of Labor Statistics

Data processing is a field with much growth potential for people interested in these careers. To be fully equipped for the jobs of tomorrow, you must accept the fact that change is inevitable with the exploding technology. The best advice you can follow is to study a wide range of subjects in addition to technical and business courses. Keep your horizons wide open, for the job you are trained for today may not exist tomorrow. Make learning an ongoing priority so that you can adjust to change as it occurs.

THE ROAD TO SUCCESS

Carefully plan your career goals and work towards reaching them. Looking for a first job can be very disheartening and frustrating, but do not let it discourage you from pursuing your ambitions. Be realistic and be prepared to work at some tasks that may not be to your liking. Perfection is hard to find. Remember that this job is only the beginning of the road to a career of your choice. Use every opportunity to show initiative and to work cooperatively with your coworkers. Look at disappointments as learning experiences and face every challenge with optimism.

> "Success in life is a matter not so much of talent or opportunity as of concentration and perseverance."
>
> C. W. Wendte

BIBLIOGRAPHY AND RECOMMENDED READING

"AARP Survey Debunks Negative Myths About Workers Over 50," *Senior World,* April 1986, p. 12.

Anderson, Avis O. and Audrey Harrigan, "Investigation of the Status of Shorthand in Business and Education," Shorthand Teachers' Association of Business Education Association of Metropolitan New York, May 14, 1988.

Angerosa, Angela M., "Secretaries Come of Age in the Eighties," *The Secretary,* June/July 1988, p. 11.

Austin, William M. and Lawrence C. Drake, Jr., "Office Automation, " *Occupational Outlook Quarterly,* Spring, 1985, p. 19.

Automation of America's Offices, Office of Technology Assessment, 1985, p. 300.

"Average Entry-Level Clerical Salaries Rise," *The Secretary,* April 1988, p. 5.

Bentley, Donald D., "A Portrait of WP in Transition," *Words,* October-November-December 1987, pp. 33-35.

Bolles, Richard Nelson, *What Color Is Your Parachute?* Ten Speed Press, 1988.

"The Career Planning Cycle: Developing a Sensible Strategy," *1986 Computer Salary Survey and Career Planning Guide,* Source EDP Personnel Services, 1986, p. 7.

Chaney, Lillian H. and Joseph Clair Otto, "Are Schools Meeting Needs of the Business Community?" *Business Education Forum,* February 1988, pp. 23-24.

"Change and the Secretary of the Future," *Networking,* Winter 1988, p. 1.

"Computers Ease the Load—At Times," *The New York Times,* August 4, 1985.

Computers in the Workplace: Selected Issues, National Commission for Employment Policy, Report No. 19, March 1986, pp. 1-2.

Costello, Cynthia B., "Technological Change and Unionization in the Service Sector," *Monthly Labor Review,* Bureau of Labor Statistics, August 1987, p. 46.

Crawford, Bill, *AARP News Bulletin,* Washington, D.C., February 1986, p. 1.

Databook: Perspectives on Working Women, U.S. Department of Labor, Bulletin 2080, October 1980.

The Dictionary of Occupational Titles, Supplement 1986 and Fourth Edition, U.S. Department of Labor, Employment and Training Administration, 1977.

Dougherty, Philip H. "Women Are Moving Up In One Area," *The New York Times,* June 1, 1988, D21.

Dworetsky, Ephraim D., "Trends in the Accounting Profession: A Summation of Controversies and Perspectives," *BEA Journal,* Spring 1988, p. 11.

Dykeman, John B., "The Fall and Rise of Word Processing," *Modern Office Technology,* November 1987, p. 14.

Employment and Earnings, Department of Labor, November 1982 and July 1987.

Erickson, Richard C. and Yves A. Asselin, "Clerical Competencies for the Automated Office of the Future," *Journal of Education for Business,* April 1986, p. 326.

"Facsimile Offers More and Experts Tell Us Why," *Office Systems '88,* May 1988, p. 44.

"Fountains of Opportunity," *The Secretary,* August/September 1987, p. 21.

Fusselman, Kay, "Job Market for Secretaries Exceptionally Strong," *The Secretary,* January 1988, p. 14.

Fusselman, Kay, "Secretaries: A Profile," *The Secretary,* August/September 1987, pp. 9-10.

Hall-Sheehy, Jim, "The Human Cost of Computing," *Information Center,* May 1988, nd.

"How Much $ Do DPers Make?" *Software News,* July 1984, p. 46.

Jones, Art, "Records Management Now & in the Future," *Office Systems '88,* May 1988, p. 100.

"The Kelly Report on People in the Electronic Office III: The Secretary's Role," Research & Forecasts, Inc., 1984.

Kerr, Susan, "Is the Computer Fostering a More Just Justice System?" *Datamation,* January 15, 1988, pp. 46, 48.

Kirby, Margaret S. and J. Dale Oliver, "Information Processing Specialist: A Redefinition of the Administrative Support Function," *The Delta Pi Epsilon Journal,* Winter 1988, pp. 14-24.

Kleinschrod, Walter A., "The Trend to Electronic Training," *Administrative Management,* April 1988, p. 29.

Lander, Estelle, "Lena Horne Knows Well the Importance of 1st Job," *Newsday,* March 23, 1988, p. 21.

Leontief, Wassily and Faye Duchin, "The Impact of Automation on Employment," 1963–2000, New York Institute for Economic Analysis, New York University, 1984.

Low, Charlotte, "Shorthand's Fading Mark," *Insight on the News,* April 25, 1988, pp. 48, 49.

Mark, Jerome A., "BLS Reports on Technological Change and Employment," *News,* Bureau of Labor Statistics, United States Department of Labor, USDL 87-150, April 17, 1987.

Naisbitt, John and Patricia Aburdene, *Reinventing the Corporation,* Warner Books, Inc., 1985.

National Survey of Professional, Administrative, Technical, and Clerical Pay, Bureau of Labor Statistics, Washington, D.C., Bulletin 2271, October 1986.

Nielson, Robert, "Partnerships that Help the Economy," *Consensus,* April 1988, p. 16.

"1987 AMS Contract Labor Survey," *The Secretary,* October 1987, p. 6.

"NSA Prototype Secretarial Job Description," *The Secretary,* May 1978, p. 38, 5, 21.

Occupational Outlook Handbook, 1986–87 edition, U.S. Department of Labor, Bureau of Labor Statistics.

Occupational Outlook Quarterly, U.S. Department of Labor, Spring, 1988, pp. 10, 12, 14.

"Office Automation and You," *The Office Professional,* January 15, 1988, pp. 6–7.

"Office Work and Minorities," *Automation of America's Offices,* December 1985, pp. 302–304.

Rose, Ginger A., "Finding the Correct Balance Between Concepts and Technology in High School Accounting," *Business Education World,* Spring 1988, pp. 27–28.

Samson, Richard W., "Telecommuting: The New Way to Work," *High Tech Careers,* October 1985, p. 15.

The Secretary, October 1987, p. 12.

Silvestri, George T. and John M. Lukasiewicz, "A Look at Occupational Enrollment Trends to the Year 2000," *Monthly Labor Review,* September 1987, pp. 46–61.

Springer, T. J., "Improving Productivity in the Workplace," Springer Associates, Inc., 1986, pp. 55–56.

"State of the Profession," *The Secretary,* August/September 1987, p. 21.

Statistical Abstract of the United States 1987, p. 388.

Stevenson, Paul A., "Employers Teaching English to Their Immigrant Workers," *The New York Times,* June 23, 1988, pp. 1 D6, Col. 3.

Strassman, Paul A., "Knowledge Management: Opportunity for the

Secretary of the Future," *The Secretary,* June/July 1987, p. 14.

Thomas, Ed., ed., *Newsletter,* Office Systems Research Association, January 1988, p. 3.

Verity, John W., "Minis, Micros, and Maturity," *Datamation,* November 1, 1986, pp. 72, 74.

Vreeland, Eleanor P., "Today's Secretary: Moving Up," *The Secretary,* June/July 1988, p. 14–17.

Women at Work, National Commission on Working Women, Spring/Summer 1986.

Workforce 2000, U.S. Department of Labor, 1987.

"Working Mother is Now Norm," *The New York Times,* June 16, 1988, p. A19.

VGM CAREER BOOKS

OPPORTUNITIES IN

Available in both paperback and hardbound editions

Accounting Careers
Acting Careers
Advertising Careers
Agriculture Careers
Airline Careers
Animal and Pet Care
Appraising Valuation Science
Architecture
Automotive Service
Banking
Beauty Culture
Biological Sciences
Book Publishing Careers
Broadcasting Careers
Building Construction Trades
Business Communication Careers
Business Management
Cable Television
Carpentry Careers
Chemical Engineering
Chemistry Careers
Child Care Careers
Chiropractic Health Care
Civil Engineering Careers
Commercial Art and Graphic Design
Computer Aided Design and Computer Aided Mfg.
Computer Maintenance Careers
Computer Science Careers
Counseling & Development
Crafts Careers
Dance
Data Processing Careers
Dental Care
Drafting Careers
Electrical Trades
Electronic and Electrical Engineering
Energy Careers
Engineering Technology Careers
Environmental Careers
Fashion Careers
Federal Government Careers
Film Careers
Financial Careers
Fire Protection Services
Fitness Careers
Food Services
Foreign Language Careers
Forestry Careers
Gerontology Careers
Government Service
Graphic Communications
Health and Medical Careers
High Tech Careers
Home Economics Careers
Hospital Administration
Hotel & Motel Management
Industrial Design
Insurance Careers
Interior Design
International Business
Journalism Careers
Landscape Architecture
Laser Technology
Law Careers
Law Enforcement and Criminal Justice
Library and Information Science
Machine Trades
Magazine Publishing Careers
Management
Marine & Maritime Careers
Marketing Careers
Materials Science
Mechanical Engineering
Microelectronics
Modeling Careers
Music Careers
Nursing Careers
Nutrition Careers
Occupational Therapy Careers
Office Occupations
Opticianry
Optometry
Packaging Science
Paralegal Careers
Paramedical Careers
Part-time & Summer Jobs
Personnel Management
Pharmacy Careers
Photography
Physical Therapy Careers
Plumbing & Pipe Fitting
Podiatric Medicine
Printing Careers
Psychiatry
Psychology
Public Health Careers
Public Relations Careers
Real Estate
Recreation and Leisure
Refrigeration and Air Conditioning
Religious Service
Retailing
Robotics Careers
Sales Careers
Sales & Marketing
Secretarial Careers
Securities Industry
Social Work Careers
Speech-Language Pathology Careers
Sports & Athletics
Sports Medicine
State and Local Government
Teaching Careers
Technical Communications
Telecommunications
Television and Video Careers
Theatrical Design & Production
Transportation Careers
Travel Careers
Veterinary Medicine Careers
Vocational and Technical Careers
Word Processing
Writing Careers
Your Own Service Business

CAREERS IN
Accounting
Business
Communications
Computers
Health Care
Science

CAREER DIRECTORIES
Careers Encyclopedia
Occupational Outlook Handbook

CAREER PLANNING
How to Get and Get Ahead On Your First Job
How to Get People to Do Things Your Way
How to Have a Winning Job Interview
How to Land a Better Job
How to Write a Winning Résumé
Joyce Lain Kennedy's Career Book
Life Plan
Planning Your Career Change
Planning Your Career of Tomorrow
Planning Your College Education
Planning Your Military Career
Planning Your Own Home Business
Planning Your Young Child's Education

SURVIVAL GUIDES
High School Survival Guide
College Survival Guide

VGM Career Horizons
a division of *NTC Publishing Group*
4255 West Touhy Avenue
Lincolnwood, Illinois 60646-1975

HD
8039
.M39
E77
1989

11.95

HD
8039
.M39
E77

1989